9/14

Bring Back the Bureaucrats

Bring Back the Bureaucrats

><

Why More Federal Workers Will Lead to Better (and Smaller!) Government

John J. DiIulio Jr.

Templeton Press
300 Conshohocken State Road, Suite 500
West Conshohocken, PA 19428
www.templetonpress.org

Designed and typeset by Gopa & Ted2, Inc.

Library of Congress Cataloging-in-Publication Data

DiIulio, John J., Jr., 1958-
  Bring back the bureaucrats : why more federal workers will lead
to better (and smaller!) government / John J. DiIulio Jr.
    pages cm
  Includes bibliographical references.
  ISBN 978-1-59947-467-0 (alk. paper)
  1. Administrative agencies—United States—Management.
  2. Bureaucracy—United States. 3. Civil service—United States .
  4. Public administration--United States. 5. Government productivity
—United States. I. Title.
  JK421.D55 2014
  331.7'6135173--dc23

                                                    2014027492

Printed in the United States of America

14 15 16 17 18 19   10 9 8 7 6 5 4 3 2 1

To Donald F. Kettl

America's foremost public administration scholar—
A great teacher, a loyal friend, and a dear man

✂

Contents

Acknowledgments

— ❥❧ —

I HAVE LEARNED ABOUT American government and public administration (or "bureaucracy") from many great scholars, but I am especially lucky to have learned from these eight: Jack H. Nagel, Henry Teune, Jameson W. Doig, Gerald J. "Gerry" Garvey, Richard P. "Dick" Nathan, Mark H. Moore, James Q. Wilson, and Donald F. Kettl.

Nearly forty years ago, I took my first bureaucracy course with Jack at the University of Pennsylvania. I was hooked. Jack was my main undergraduate mentor, and he became my Penn colleague, dean, and comrade in sustaining the Master of Public Administration (MPA) program at Penn's Fels Institute of Government. Jack is a gentle genius, and his wise counsel, both personal and professional, are among my life's treasures. I also took several undergraduate classes with Henry, plus a de facto graduate seminar on research methods that he offered to me during weekly one-on-one office hours that ran several hours each week. I was reunited with Henry when I left Princeton for Penn, and we coadvised several students on public administration–type theses or dissertations; by rights I should have paid Henry tuition, because he never stopped teaching me.

I cotaught the core MPA public management course at Princeton's Woodrow Wilson School with Jameson, an unfailingly kind and generous colleague whose disagreements with my views on crime and corrections resulted only in wonderful discussions and whose seminal work on public leadership and innovation repays reading to this day. As with Jameson, I cotaught and also did training for federal workers with Gerry, who helped to inform the very best of the thinking and writing about public administration that I did while at Princeton, including my essay on the federal government's "principled agents."[1] He was not only the single most eclectically brilliant person I have ever known (from math to constitutional theory to you name it), but also smart with heart in profound ways that come across in much of his underappreciated work, including his monumental case study of a federal agency and the amazing public administration textbook that he published just a few years before he died.[2]

I also cotaught Princeton's core public management MPA course with Dick and later collaborated with him on Brookings books on health care administration and also a field network study involving government partnerships with religious nonprofit organizations. Our collaboration continues. Even as he nears his eightieth birthday, I have to race just to keep up with him as we proceed with our ongoing national study of the implementation of the Patient Protection and Affordable Care Act, better known as the ACA or Obamacare. And the only person to rival Dick for the title of the most inspiring and public-spirited academic I know is Mark. I never took a course with Mark, and we never served on the same faculty together (not counting my stint a few years ago as a visiting professor at the Harvard Kennedy School). He pioneered and led the "executive sessions" that helped to revolutionize thinking about policing in America. That is just one such remarkable, real-world accomplishment among many that are all to his great and lasting credit. His mentorship and scholarship have enlivened and leavened my thinking for more than three decades now, and his writing about "creating public value" is and shall remain the gold standard for creative and public-spirited public management scholarship.

Jim Wilson was my mentor for thirty-two years, including two decades during which I had the honor to be the coauthor of his magnificent American government textbook. He often beckoned me to revise his 1989 magnum opus *Bureaucracy: What Government Agencies Do and Why They Do It* and to publish it as my own. I never took him up on that absurdly generous offer, but, in the year before he died, I did promise him that I would publish an article summarizing my thinking on "big intergovernment and its private administrative proxies." I did,[3] and he lived long enough to read and comment on it. I also promised him that I would get around to researching and writing a weighty scholarly tome on the subject that might make him proud.

In 2012, shortly after Jim died, my friend (and fellow Philly-bred boy) Peter Dougherty, editor-in-chief at Princeton University Press, signed me up to do that book. It is tentatively entitled *The Daddy State: Facing Up to Big Government*; it should be in Pete's hands (and will be dedicated to Jim) in 2015. Templeton Press's Susan Arellano worked with Pete at Free Press back in the days when it was led by the great Erwin Glikes. Erwin, for whom I did my first book, *Governing Prisons: A Comparative Study of Correctional Management*, in 1987, used to talk about a book becoming "the text of the debate" on a given issue. From my work on religion and faith-based initiatives, I have known many folks at the John Templeton Foundation for years. But I did not know Susan. In 2013, she had a bug about me doing a book on "bureaucracy" planted in her ear by Yuval Levin, editor of *National Affairs* and the most insightful young conservative thinker in America today (thanks, Yuval). She reached out to me. She suggested, and Pete agreed, that the debate on "big government" was big enough for two texts on the topic. They jointly conceived the present book as a crystallization of certain core concerns and prescriptions, and the next book as an attempt to refine, extend, and deepen the analysis and prescriptions in relation to the literature on American political development that, as I conceive it, begins not with late twentieth-century political science but with the nineteenth-century observer of American democracy (and its penitentiaries!), Alexis de Tocqueville.

So, I am very grateful to Pete, and I am thankful and indebted to Susan for hatching the idea of doing this book and for all her editorial TLC. Her firm but gentle hand kept me from writing a much (much) longer book (Pete's!), and she persuaded me to take her counsel on the present book's prescriptive title: bring back the bureaucrats indeed! I am also indebted to Susan's Templeton Press colleague, Trish Vergilio, for shepherding me through an expedited editing and production process with southern charm and northern efficiency; thanks, Trish.

But without Donald F. Kettl, neither I nor anyone else would have such general, meaningful, and true knowledge about the state of American government and public administration. In 1988, the year before Jim Wilson published *Bureaucracy*, Don published *Government by Proxy: (Mis?)Managing Federal Programs*. In the mid-1990s, when I directed the Brookings Center for Public Management, I had the extreme privilege and pleasure of working closely with Don and being his coauthor or coeditor on numerous books and published reports. I learned then and since that, when it comes to anything (anything!) that touches the topic of public administration at home or abroad, Don knows everything including, and most importantly, what we do not yet know.

I must acknowledge just one little example of so many. During Don's too-brief time at Penn, before he left to become the dean of the University of Maryland's School of Public Policy, I began to get interested in the fact that, at least in Philly, faith-based organizations (mainly Catholic-affiliated ones) played what seemed like a fairly robust role in the administration of the summer food and nutrition entitlement programs of the U.S. Department of Agriculture (USDA). I began to wonder more broadly about how the programs were administered. Don told me straight off what it took me two years to "discover" for myself: there is no way to get a wholly reliable, real-time handle *either* on all the federal, state, and local government agencies and their full-time or part-time employees, *or* on all the nongovernment organizations and individuals paid on whatever basis by whichever government agencies or via whichever intergovernmental funding sources, *or* on all the unpaid groups and individuals that, at any given moment, might constitute the federal programs' proxy-laden and proxy-layered administrative apparatus.

Upon this discovery, it dawned on me (as it had not done since my earliest days studying how differences in prison management relate to differences in the quality of life behind bars) that public administration matters; it *really* matters. In this case, millions of poor kids in America needlessly went hungry each summer because of the crazy-quilt way we administer this one federal entitlement program.

Don answered my research aspirations and "it really matters" revelations with his warm, knowing, encouraging smile. He rattled off detailed, professorial suggestions. And he offered both personal and professional assurances that getting even a semifirm handle on the programs' proxy administration in Philly alone might prove well worth the effort in both intellectual and civic terms. With a bunch of students and several Penn colleagues, led by Joseph P. Tierney (thanks, Joe), that is what I did, and Penn picked up a USDA award along the way for building a website that helps the parents or guardians of eligible children find the summer program site nearest to their homes; that is your award, too, Don.

So, in addition to all the best work that Don and I did together at Brookings back in the 1990s, I owe not only the foundational concepts and far-reaching ideas about proxy government that inform this book, but also numerous research forays and "live action" public administration problem-solving projects to Don's towering intellect, timely guidance, and generous spirit.

That said, I alone am responsible for the arguments, illustrations, and prescriptions in this book; blame me for whatever herein you find objectionable or worse, and credit Don and the other good friends and mentors that I have acknowledged for anything herein that you might pronounce either valuable or good.

Bring Back the Bureaucrats

Introduction

—— ✥ ——

I LOVE AMERICAN government. I better. Over the last three decades, I have lectured about it as a professor at three Ivy League universities; studied it as a scholar and research center director at several public policy think tanks; written about it as the coauthor of a leading textbook on the subject; and witnessed it up close as a senior White House official.

As I see it, American government is neither perfect nor pretty, but it is nonetheless majestic and miraculous. The bold experiment in "government by reflection and choice"[1] that began more than two centuries ago in Philadelphia (my beloved hometown) is still underway. In more ways than the Constitution's authors dared to dream, it worked. I have seen the Capitol Dome a zillion times, but each time I see it, I still get a little lump in my throat to match the one I get whenever I walk or drive by Independence Hall in Philadelphia.

But, too often now, I get a different sort of lump in my throat—the choking kind—when I hear about what is happening in Washington, read about the latest government financial follies, or research the latest federal policy spectacle (coleading a major national study of the implementation of the Patient Protection and Affordable Care Act of 2010, also known as the ACA or Obamacare, has only heightened my concerns).

And I know that my millennial generation college students are also listening, watching, and tweeting. They are looking to their baby boomer elders for a moral compass, practical guidance, and cut-to-the-core honesty and frankness. No less than previous generations, they have indulged my love for American history and constitutional theories, but they have also pushed me harder than any previous generation has done when it comes to telling them what I really think and feel about the present state of American government. They have asked what, if anything, might be done to make it work better and be a blessing to "ourselves and our Posterity."

Thus, I am writing this book in a patriotic and pedagogical spirit that compels me to be brutally frank and honest about how American government really works; to speak unpopular truths about how "We the People" have degraded our government and ourselves; to advance a provocatively counterintuitive but robustly factual thesis about how to trim, tame, and improve government; to prescribe far-reaching reforms that will, at least on first hearing, be selectively rejected by many libertarians and by many liberals; and to pray for nothing less than a public epiphany about "big government" that transcends ideological and partisan divides and forces those who seek national office in 2014 and thereafter to face up to damning fiscal *and* administrative realities that have been hiding in plain view for decades.

Compared to today's American government, the Roman emperors' bread and circuses were honest democratic leadership in action. Post-1960 leaders in both parties have won and kept office by behaving as if Washington can "do something" or "do more" about nearly everything (health care, environmental protection, crime, poverty, education, national defense, homeland security, and more), and can dispense ever greater benefits to ever more people, without requiring their constituents to pay more (or pay at all) for the new or expanded government services *and* without hiring more full-time federal bureaucrats to administer them.

From the military-industrial complex to the entitlement-nonprofit complex, today's American government is a debt-financed, proxy-administered, superficially antistatist form of big government. Leveraged, not led, by Washington, America's big government works by borrowing billions of dollars each year from Americans who are not yet born and hiring millions of Americans each year who are never counted on the federal payroll. It wears two ill-fitting masks: (1) it masks its huge spending by debt financing, and (2) it masks its huge scope by employing even fewer full-time federal bureaucrats today than it did a half-century ago—the crux of my concern in this book. Big government funds state and local government employees, for-profit business contractors, and nonprofit organization grantees to administer federal policies, programs, and regulations. In some federal policy domains, it also mandates but does not fund subnational government employees to function as de facto federal employees; and in many federal policy domains, it relies heavily on networks of grantees, subgrantees, contractors, and subcontractors mustered by subnational governments.

As I explain and illustrate throughout this book, today's American government is "Leviathan by Proxy," a grotesque form of big government that guarantees bad government:

- It does not spend less than the governments of many ostensibly more "statist" European democracies, and it leaves no area of social or economic life untouched (or unregulated).
- It cannot predictably, reliably, or cost-effectively do what democratically enacted public laws dictate that it must, whether that is collecting taxes, cleaning up toxic waste sites, supplying eligible low-income children with meals during the summer, getting major weapons systems delivered on time and within budget, ending improper health care payments, etc.
- It results in too few federal "acquisition workforce" bureaucrats chasing too many proxies, monitoring too many grants and contracts, and handling too many dollars; beyond well-publicized implosions like those that defined the response to Hurricane Katrina in 2005 and

the launch of Obamacare health exchanges in 2013, it routinely courts administrative meltdowns on chores as distinct as caring for hospitalized veterans, handling plutonium, and approving pesticides.

- It frustrates far-reaching "government performance and results" reforms: in addition to the sheer administrative complexity, well-documented program duplication, fragmentation, cost overruns, and other inefficiencies persist in part because many federal policies, programs, and regulations are a province of multiple and competing proxies cum "vendors" with political clout that stretches from the lawmaking process to the procurement process.

- It undercuts public administration's democratic accountability by making the implementation of most federal policies, programs, and regulations so vastly complicated and varied that it takes teams of researchers just to begin to describe—not analyze or evaluate, just describe—which federal agency or agencies, and which, if any, other groups (including subnational government agencies, for-profit contractors or subcontractors, nonprofit organization grantees or subgrantees, or, in the case of many human services programs, individual citizens and volunteers) are actively involved, what they actually do, and how they actually do it.[2]

- It fosters nonstop government growth as Washington's proxies—state and local government officials (both elected and appointed), heads of for-profit corporations, and leaders of nonprofit organizations—incessantly advocate or outright lobby for federal policies, programs, and regulations that they administer or coadminister.

As I argue in this book's concluding chapter, many measures are needed to reform our government. If we want to pump the brakes on big government's expansion while improving its performance, then we must start by pruning the system's proxies while increasing the federal workforce. To undercut the proxy-bred political pressures behind government's growth and to bolster government performance (or at least to avert near-term administrative debacles in indisputably understaffed federal agencies), we must indeed "bring back the bureaucrats."

As I argue in this book's second chapter, if there is one institution to blame for the deranged state of contemporary American government and "public administration," it is the incumbent-dominated Congress. In recent years, for example, in the name of "rightsizing the federal workforce," some House Republican leaders have pushed for new laws that would allow federal agencies to hire just one full-time employee for every two that leave the federal service.[3] But, make no mistake: many such proposals have a bipartisan pedigree.

In 2010, a bipartisan presidential commission noted that the federal government "employs about two million people, and extends federal staffing through thousands more contractors."[4] As I document in this book, the truth is that the ratios of federal bureaucrats to citizens, expenditures, and proxies have plummeted since 1960, and that Washington "extends federal staffing" not through thousands but through millions of contractors and other nonfederal proxies. But the "fiscal responsibility and reform" commission's report called for reducing the federal civilian workforce by 10 percent and "hiring only two new workers for every three who leave service."[5]

Never mind, I suppose, that simply eliminating the *entire* full-time federal civilian workforce and its payroll (about $250 billion a year in wages and benefits) would save less than the federal government now spends each year just on Medicare beneficiaries (about $600 billion), and less than it now spends each year just on for-profit defense contractors (more than $300 billion); and never mind that having zero federal bureaucrats might just pose a slight problem in getting Medicare benefits claims processed and defense contracts managed and monitored.

I know, therefore, that this book, filled though it is with facts, figures, and footnoted examples, is also filled with arguments and prescriptions that are not anywhere in season. But, being as I am a pro-life and pro-poor Catholic Democrat, I am used to feeling like a person without an ideological posse or an all-embracing party.

Besides, each of my two favorite intellectual architects of American government, James Madison and Alexander

Hamilton, offers encouragement. Madison reminds us that in experimenting with constitutional government and addressing its present-day problems, each generation of Americans must rely on "the suggestions of their own good sense" and "the knowledge of their own situation."⁶And Hamilton, in words that should convict us, insists that "a government ill executed, whatever it may be in theory, must be, in practice, a bad government."⁷

I wrote this book because "good sense" and "knowledge of our situation" demands that we finally face up to the whole truth about today's "ill-executed" American government and commence the battle of ideas and wills necessary to making it good again.

Part 1

※

Bring Back the Bureaucrats

Leviathan by Proxy

><

EVERYONE KNOWS that America's federal government has grown bigger and bigger over the last half-century. In 2013, Washington spent more than $3.5 trillion. Adjusted for inflation, that was five times more than it spent in 1960. Indeed, the roughly $6 trillion in federal budget deficits that Washington amassed from 2009 to 2013 exceeded total federal spending for the period 1960 through 1966. While annual federal budget deficits are now projected to average "only" about $500 billion a year from 2014 through 2018, Washington's financial problems remain far from solved. For instance, Medicare, the federal health insurance program that covers most senior citizens, has an unfunded, long-term liability of about $40 trillion.[1]

Still, the big story about big government that matters most to America's future is not all about Washington's finances. It's not captured by the usual partisan and ideological debates. And it's dimly perceived and barely understood even by most academics who make their living by studying American government and public policy.

The really big story about big government in America can be glimpsed by eyeballing the figure that appears on this book's cover.[2] In constant 2013 dollars, annual federal government spending doubled between 1960 and 1975. It then doubled again between 1975 and 2005. This expansion in federal spending was accompanied by an expansion of the federal bureaucracy. Since 1965, six new federal cabinet agencies have been established (including, most recently, the Department of Homeland Security in 2002), many new sub-cabinet agencies have been created (for example, the Environmental Protection Agency in 1970), and the total number of pages in the *Federal Register*, which catalogues federal government policies, programs, and regulations, has increased about fourfold (to more than 80,000 pages).

And yet, during the same half-century that federal government spending increased fivefold, the number of federal bureaucrats increased hardly at all.

In fact, during several post-1960 periods when federal spending spiked and new federal cabinet departments and agencies launched, the number of full-time federal civil servants, excluding uniformed military personnel and postal workers, actually *decreased*.

When George W. Bush won the presidency in 2000, as when John F. Kennedy won it in 1960, the executive branch employed about 1.8 million full-time civilian workers. And when Ronald Reagan won reelection in 1984, there were slightly *more* federal bureaucrats (about 2.2 million) than when Barack Obama won reelection in 2012 (about 2 million).

Using constant 2013 dollars, in 1960, the federal government spent about $726 billion and employed about 1.8 million full-time federal bureaucrats; in 1975, the federal government spent about $1.4 trillion and employed 2.1 million full-time bureaucrats. Thus, between 1960 and 1975, Washington's annual spending increased by about 200 percent, but its full-time workforce increased by less than 20 percent. By 2005, Washington spent around $2.9 trillion, which was about four times as much as it spent in 1960. But in 2005, as in 1960, there were about 1.8 million full-time federal civilian bureaucrats: federal spending was about four times larger, but the federal workforce was about the same size. Indeed, the full-time federal civilian workforce was actually smaller in 2013 than it was in twenty-six of the fifty-three years since 1960.

Washington now spends billions of dollars a year on home-land security, housing, environmental protection, elementary education, child welfare services, health care, urban transportation, and much more. Today's federal government has laws, policies, programs, bureaucracies, and regulations on numerous matters that were not on the federal agenda (or

were barely on it) when Dwight D. Eisenhower was president. Even though it now leaves no area of American life
untouched, the federal government with its multitrillion-
dollar annual budget has roughly the same number of full-
time federal bureaucrats today as it had when Ike left office.

But how?

"Big government" in America is a Washington-led big
*inter*government *by proxy*. This fundamental truth about
how big government in America really works has been hiding in plain view for decades. Big intergovernment's proxies
are state and local governments, for-profit businesses, and
nonprofit organizations.

State and Local Government Proxies

- More than two dozen federal departments and agencies
  spend a combined total of more than $600 billion a year
  on more than 200 intergovernmental grant programs for
  state and local governments.[3]
- Adjusted for inflation, between 1960 and 2012, federal
  grants-in-aid to states increased more than tenfold.[4]
- Over the last half-century, while the federal civilian workforce remained around 2 million full-time bureaucrats, the
  total number of state and local government employees
  roughly tripled to more than 18 million.
- In 2011, there were 14.8 million full-time and 4.8 million part-time workers employed by state and local
  governments.[5]

- The single largest budget item in most state budgets is Medicaid, a means-tested federal-state program that pays the medical expenses of persons receiving federal welfare or supplemental security income payments. In 2011, Washington spent about $275 billion and states spent about $157 billion on Medicaid; the federal government paid at least half of the states' administrative costs for Medicaid.[6]

For-Profit Business Proxies

- The federal government spends more than $500 billion a year on contracts with for-profit firms.[7] Many for-profit firms, from small businesses to huge corporations, have the federal government as a major or sole customer.
- In 2012, the Department of Defense (DOD) obligated roughly $350 billion to contractors. The DOD had about 800,000 DOD civilian workers plus the equivalent of some 710,000 full-time contract employees.[8]
- The federal government's DOD-anchored military-industrial complex is a first cousin to its entitlement-industrial complex involving both for-profit and nonprofit proxies.
- With more than 300 different federal programs, the Department of Health and Human Services is not only the single largest federal grant-making agency (81,000 grants totaling nearly $350 billion in 2012), but it is the third largest federal contracting agency ($19 billion in contracts in 2013).[9]

- All told, in 2012, businesses that received federal contracts employed an estimated 22 percent of the U.S. workforce, or about 26 million workers.[10]
- From Superfund to Social Security, from child welfare services to nuclear safety services, there is virtually no federal government domestic policy, program, or regulation that is untouched by for-profit contractors.

Nonprofit Organization Proxies

- The nonprofit sector encompasses about 1.6 million organizations registered with the Internal Revenue Service plus many thousands more tax-exempt organizations that are not required to register and opt not to do so.
- The subset of nonprofit organizations that filed reports with the IRS (about 40 percent of all registered nonprofits) has about $2 trillion in annual revenues, and roughly a third of the money comes from government grants plus fees for services and goods from government sources.[11]
- In 2012, governments entered into about 350,000 contracts and grants with about 56,000 nonprofit organizations (an average of six contracts/grants per nonprofit organization) and paid $137 billion to nonprofit organizations for services.[12]
- Billions of dollars in federal "pass-through grants" flow from Washington through state capitals and into the coffers of local governments and nonprofit organizations.

In 2012, Washington supplied nearly $80 billion in such grants.[13]

- In 2010, the nonprofit sector employed about 10.7 percent of the U.S. workforce, or nearly 11 million people—the nation's third largest workforce behind only retail trade and manufacturing.[14]

- In addition to receiving government grants and fees, many nonprofit organizations own tax-exempt properties, receive tax-deductible donations, and have beneficiaries or clients who receive tax-funded payments, subsidies, or loans with which to "purchase" the nonprofit organization's goods or services.[15]

- In the late 1990s and early 2000s, my own fairly well-known case for federal "faith-based initiatives" and "leveling the playing field" was essentially about ensuring that urban congregations and small, community-serving religious nonprofit groups were eligible for federal and intergovernmental grants or contracts on the same basis as other nonprofit organizations, both religious and secular, that had long received such grants and contracts.[16]

Not without good reason, the rise of "big government" is commonly discussed in relation to record public spending and public debt. In recent years, federal government spending has averaged about 24 percent of gross domestic product (GDP)[17] and combined state and local government spending has averaged around 16 percent of GDP.[18] After reaching 27 percent in 1960, total government spending (federal plus state and local) in the United States as a percentage of GDP remained in the thirties in most years from 1980 through the mid-2000s, but it increased to 42 percent in 2009, and by the early 2010s, it hovered around 40 percent.[19]

At roughly 40 percent, America's government spending to GDP ratio rivals that of many European democracies. Indeed, adjusted for cross-national differences in health insurance accounting practices, it has been estimated that total government spending in the United States as a percentage of GDP (46.8 percent) is just a couple points below the average for the seventeen so-called Euro Area democracies (49.3 percent).[20]

By the same token, federal government debt per capita is about $53,000, and total government spending (federal, state, and local) per capita is about $19,000—a total of more than $70,000 a year in government finances for each man, woman, and child in the country.[21] In recent years, both America's per capita government spending and its debt-to-GDP ratio were actually higher than those of many European democracies.[22]

Thus, America's big government does not spend or borrow significantly less than all the supposedly more "statist" European democracies do. Rather, what is most distinctive about big government or "the state" in America is not how much it spends or borrows, but how the nation's policies, programs, and regulations are administered.

Most European democracies restrict "outsourcing" far

more than the United States does. For example, German law dictates that all persons involved in administering national policies must be directly supervised by a government official, and in France, the United Kingdom, and most other European democracies, there are either constitutional, statutory, or customary limits that favor direct public administration. The same is true for Japan and many other non-European democracies.

Uniquely, big government in America is *Leviathan by Proxy*. Following are just a few brief examples:

- The Patient Protection and Affordable Care Act of 2010, also known as the ACA or Obamacare, is a big-government program that uses contractors by the dozens (including both for-profit firms and nonprofit organizations) that have been paid by the U.S. Department of Health and Human Services or the U.S. Department of the Treasury to build information technology systems, help consumers navigate the health exchange marketplaces, and more.[23] As the Health and Human Services Office of the Inspector General has noted, "Contractors have played, and will continue to play, a vital role in building, maintaining, and fixing the computer systems that underpin the implementation" of the ACA and its health "exchanges."[24]

- At one point the Department of Homeland Security had more private contract employees (about 200,000) than federal employees (about 188,000).[25] It has distributed hundreds of billions of dollars to cities, big and small, and allocated the funds by the same so-called fair-share formulas that Congress uses to allocate certain highway funds among the states. Between 2001 and today, more than 500 private companies specializing in "security and counterterrorism" have come into being; many of the 1,400 for-profit firms in that industry that existed prior to 2001 have expanded via federal funding.[26]

- The Department of Agriculture administers its summer food and nutrition entitlement programs through a mazelike network of state government agencies, local government agencies, nonprofit organizations, and stipend-receiving individual citizens.[27]

- The Environmental Protection Agency relies heavily on for-profit firms and other proxies to identify and treat the roughly 3,400 toxic waste sites on its "national priorities list."[28]

- The Department of Energy spends 90 percent of its annual budget on contracts and pays for-profit firms to implement all programs, including its most important and high-risk ones (like the Plutonium Disposition Program).[29]

- For decades now, the aforementioned Medicaid program, including its long-term care in nursing homes, has been administered mainly by state government agencies via state government employees and their for-profit contractors and nonprofit grantees.[30]

In the 1990s, the Clinton administration created mantras about "reinventing government" and "making government work better and cost less." But, over the last two decades, government performance has not improved significantly, and the federal bureaucracy has not been "reinvented." Putting aside sweeping claims regarding "waste, fraud, and abuse," there are scores of well-documented cases of federal agency fragmentation, overlap, duplication, and forgone cost-savings.[31] Washington and the federal bureaucracy are among the last places most people would look for administrative best practices. Here are just a few tips of this iceberg:

- $125.4 billion in "improper payments" made by 70 federal programs spread across 20 different agencies (counting just a subset of all federal programs) made in 2010 alone.[32]
- Scores of billions of dollars in improper Medicare and Medicaid payments made in each year for more than a decade now.[33]
- The famously feckless FEMA response to Hurricane Katrina in New Orleans.[34]
- The flawed Hubble Space Telescope.[35]
- Numerous scandals and failures in federal housing programs and persistent "resource management" problems at the Department of Housing and Urban Development.[36]
- Failures to monitor and manage nonprofit and for-profit clinical health providers and other contractors that do work for the Department of Veterans Affairs.[37]

- Extensive noncompetitive contracting by the Department of Defense.[38]
- Chronic problems with the Department of Transportation's procurement programs and "acquisition workforce."[39]
- "Priority" toxic waste sites identified by the Environmental Protection Agency that have yet to be cleaned up.[40]
- More than $350 billion each year in Internal Revenue Service–identified taxes that go uncollected.[41]
- Spotty implementation of the Government Performance and Results Act of 1993 and the Government Performance and Results Modernization Act of 2010.[42]
- Profound implementation problems that awaited the Clinton "health alliances" plan in 1993 (problems that were averted only because the plan was never enacted).[43]
- Profound implementation problems that plagued the Obama "health exchanges" in 2013 (problems that went well beyond mere "computer glitches").[44]

But the problems go deeper than policy implementation failures or frustrated hopes for making government work better and cost less. Leviathan by Proxy reflects a derangement of our constitutional system, a loss of responsible republican representation, a decline in responsible democratic citizenship, a plague of poor public administration, and an insidious, almost irresistible, force for government growth. Here are some examples:

- Subverting the separation of powers, Congress and the federal courts, not the executive branch and the president, lead in deciding how to "faithfully execute" federal laws.
- Trivializing federalism traditions, state and local governments function ever less like sovereign civic authorities and ever more like Washington's administrative appendages.
- Hollowing James Madison's hopes for "proper guardians of the public weal,"[45] congresspersons win reelection by fighting phony ideological wars with each other, lavishing debt-financed benefits on constituents, taking campaign cash from groups that get government grant or contract dollars, and using proxy administration to shroud government's size and attenuate their accountability for its performance.
- Many for-profit businesses and nonprofit organizations relate to government as narrowly self-interested factions. For example, drug companies virtually wrote certain Obamacare provisions, and in 2011 and 2012, organizations that won federal funds to implement Obamacare spent more than $100 million on lobbying.[46]
- "We the People" demand ever-greater public benefits for ourselves, casually handing the bill for big government to our posterity while pretending not to touch Leviathan's hand.
- Even when capable, full-time federal bureaucrats strive to do a good job, they often cannot because there are simply

too few of them relative to the myriad tasks they are supposed to perform, the massive amounts of money they are responsible for disbursing, and the parades of proxies they are charged with managing and monitoring.

Leviathan by Proxy is the method behind Washington's ever-worsening madness. The public has worried about sky-high public debts, witnessed mile-high policy implementation failures, and blamed the inside-the-beltway politicians, bureaucrats, and "special interests." But the public has also wanted big-government benefits, not only without big-government taxes, but also without ever-bigger government bureaucracies. Over the last half-century, the bipartisan, safe-seat coalition on Capitol Hill, joined by both conservative Republican and liberal Democrat presidents, and with a constitutional carte blanche from the federal courts, has placated the public by using *both* debt financing *and* proxy administration to fuel government's growth while fogging it. Only in recent years, amidst debt-exploding deficits and headline-grabbing administrative debacles, has the truth about how big government in America really works become somewhat harder to avoid.

In Leviathan by Proxy, federal civil servants function mainly as grant monitors or contract compliance officers, but the bureaucrats are not the proxies' bosses. Rather, each proxy sector—state and local governments, for-profit businesses, and nonprofit organizations—has a highly active interest group presence in Washington. The proxies influence the federal policymaking process both at the front end (bills that do or do not become law) and at the back end (the administrative rules that govern how—and by whom—laws ultimately get funded and translated into administrative action).

For instance, in 2011, during a threatened (but avoided) government shutdown, the bipartisan congressional "super committee" made noises about finding ways to trim the federal budget. In response, proxy-government providers within and across every federal government policy domain were on high alert and went more public than usual. Speaking at the National Press Club, the president and CEO of the Aerospace Industry Association noted that the "industry supports 2.9 million jobs across all 50 states" and urged federal lawmakers to "consider whether eliminating hundreds of thousands of jobs over the next decade is at all consistent with the national imperative to create jobs."[47]

Echoing that plea, Independent Sector, an umbrella organization that advocates for hundreds of nonprofit leaders, rallied members and supporters to send a message to Pennsylvania's Republican senator, Pat Toomey, who was then a member of the Joint Select Committee on Deficit Reduction, better known as the "super committee." Toomey was then weighing reductions in the charitable deduction and pushing for some spending cuts. Independent Sector's recommended sample message to contact Senator Toomey read in part: "Nonprofits in Pennsylvania employ over 647,000

people, almost 12 percent of the workforce, and provide programs, goods and services to millions of people all across our
state."[48] Ten days later, another message blast stressed that "it
is imperative that members of Congress hear from you. . . .
It is important to remind them that our sector is a powerful
economic engine that employs 13 million workers."[49]

Governors, mayors, state and local government commis-
sioners, for-profit defense industry contractors, nonprofit sector grantees from secular university presidents to religious
charity executives, and others are the strange-bedfellows
lobby for Leviathan by Proxy. Whether in defense, health care,
homeland security, environmental protection, education, veteran affairs, transportation, or other areas, they hardly ever
lose, which is why government never stops growing.

CHAPTER 2

Big Brother Is Outsourcing: Leveraged, *Not* Limited, Government

‒‹

GOVERNMENT HAS GROWN and grown since 1960, but most Americans still hate "big government," right? After all, in 2013, 76 percent of Americans did not trust the federal government to do the right thing most or all the time;[1] public approval of Congress averaged about 14 percent;[2] and, for the first time, a majority of Americans believed that the federal government threatened their personal rights and freedoms.[3] In 2012, when asked to choose one of two messages to send to the federal government, 54 percent chose "leave me alone" while 35 percent chose "lend me a hand."[4]

Americans do indeed hate "big government," but, they also love, love, *love* federal government goods, services, and benefits, such as a large national defense establishment and total health care coverage for grandparents in private nursing homes, to name a few examples. As figure 1 attests, from big-budget programs like Medicaid to small-budget programs like school meals, 90-plus percent of "big government"

FIGURE 1. "BIG GOVERNMENT" PROGRAM DOLLARS: 90-PLUS PERCENT FOR BENEFICIARIES, NOT BUREAUCRACIES

■ BENEFITS AND SERVICES

■ STATE ADMINISTRATIVE COSTS

■ FEDERAL ADMINISTRATIVE COSTS

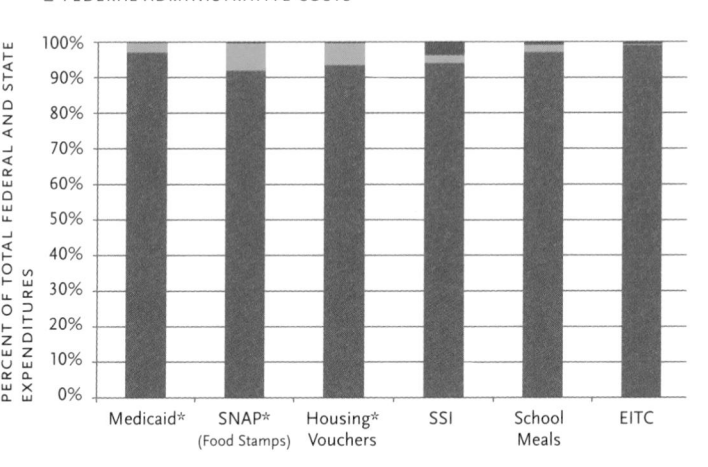

*Federal administrative costs as a percent of total federal and state expenditures for Medicaid, SNAP, and housing vouchers are just 0.1%, 0.3%, and 0.3%, respectively.

Note: SNAP=Supplemental Nutrition Assistance Program, SSI=Supplemental Security Income, EITC=Earned Income Tax Credit.

For Medicaid and SNAP, "state administrative costs" include the federal-, state-, and in some localities, county-funded shares of state administrative costs. For housing vouchers, state administrative costs include the cost of local housing agencies that operate the program. For housing vouchers, state administrative costs include the cost of local housing agencies that operate the program.

Source: Robert Greenstein and CBPP Staff, "For Major Low-Income Programs, More Than 90 Percent Goes to Beneficiaries" (Washington, DC,: Center on Budget and Policy Priorities, January 23, 2012), 2, based on the Center for Budget and Policy Priorities' analysis of data for fiscal year 2010 from the U.S. Office of Management and Budget and federal and state government agency offices.

program dollars go to beneficiaries, not to federal or state bureaucracies.

Post-1960 voters have been, and continue to be, at once philosophically conservative (they want "smaller," "less intrusive," or just plain "less" national government, and no or low taxes) and behaviorally liberal (majorities will accept no major cuts in any federal program that they believe benefits them or others with whom they identify, and most people who vote tend to vote accordingly). Thus, as the March 1, 2013, deadline for a possible federal budget sequester (mandatory spending cuts) loomed, 3 to 1 (or even wider) majorities of Americans opposed decreasing government spending on Social Security, Medicare, environmental protection, antipoverty programs, and twelve other areas; 2 to 1 majorities opposed decreasing government spending on unemployment aid and the State Department; and the only thing on which a near-majority (48 percent) favored federal spending cuts was "aid to the world's needy." In fact, as table 1 summarizes, the appetite for *increasing* government spending was greater than that for decreasing it in all but three areas (unemployment aid, State Department, and foreign aid).

Sure, most voters agree that budget deficits and the public debt are a major problem, and many like it when their leaders bash "big government." But, as all the surveys suggest, most voters are not thereby supporting real cuts in government programs. Rare is the elected leader in either party who does not read between the electorate's antigovernment sentiments

TABLE 1. FEW AMERICANS FAVOR CUTS IN GOVERNMENT SPENDING

Would you increase, decrease, or keep spending the same for	INCREASE (%)	SAME (%)	DECREASE (%)
Agriculture	34	42	20
Aid to needy in U.S.	27	44	24
Aid to world's needy	21	28	48
Anti-terrorism defenses	32	45	19
Combatting crime	41	41	14
Education	60	29	10
Energy	36	38	21
Environmental protection	33	43	22
Food and drug inspection	33	50	14
Health care	38	34	22
Medicare	36	46	15
Military defense	32	41	24
Natural disaster relief	34	50	12
Roads and infrastructure	38	43	17
Scientific research	37	40	20
Social Security	41	46	10
State Department	14	46	34
Unemployment aid	24	41	32
Veterans' benefits	53	38	6

Source: Pew Research Center for the People and the Press, "As Sequester Looms, Little Support for Cutting Most Programs" (poll, February 22, 2013, poll conducted February 13–18, 2013). http://www.people-press.org/2013/02/22/as-sequester-deadline-looms-little-support-for-cutting-most-programs/. Used by permission.

and fashion bills accordingly. One revealing case in point is the fine print in the ostensibly "far-reaching" and "conservative" Medicare reform plan cosponsored by Paul Ryan, Republican representative from Wisconsin, and thereafter the 2012 GOP nominee for vice president. Proposed on December 15, 2011, it featured a "premium support" (voucher-type) option under which beneficiaries could choose either a traditional Medicare plan or a Medicare-approved private plan. Total out-of-pocket Medicare costs were to be capped at $6,000 per person, and low-income citizens who could not pay the cap would receive a big subsidy from the government. The plan's public press release "fact sheet" was a rhapsody regarding the need "to strengthen Medicare and health security for all," with "no changes for those in or near retirement," and with a guarantee that Americans age fifty-six and older "would see no changes to the structure of their benefits."[5]

Americans hate Congress but love their respective congresspersons: from 1964 to 2012 about 93 percent of House incumbents and 82 percent of Senate incumbents who sought reelection won it; from 1980 to 2012, the House and Senate incumbent reelection rates were 94 percent and 87 percent, respectively.[6] In the 2010 midterm election, despite polls showing mass disaffection with the federal government in general and Congress in particular, 87 percent of House incumbents who sought reelection won it, as did 84 percent of Senate incumbents.[7] In 2012, among reelection-seeking incumbents, 90 percent of House incumbents and 91 percent of Senate incumbents won reelection.[8] By the same token, as careful political science studies have discerned, voters reward incumbent presidents (or their party's nominee) for increased federal spending in their local communities.[9]

Alas, Democrats are the party of "benefit more," Republicans are the party of "tax less," and, together, federal government incumbents in both parties have placated the voting public and won twenty-five consecutive national plebiscites (1964 through 2012).

Leviathan by Proxy, however, is mainly Congress's creation and creature. Congress, not the more than 3,000 presidential political appointees in the cabinet agencies nominated by the president, is the system's main author and primary master. As James Q. Wilson has explained, Congress controls the federal bureaucracy's "major day-to-day activities" and determines the "conditions within which an agency operates."[10] In every way that matters most to what federal government agencies do and why they do it, Congress, with its more than 20,000 staff members and its beehivelike "administrative oversight" committees by the dozens, "is the architect of the bureaucracy."[11] The "bureaucrats implementing" federal laws "do not merely react" to this control—"they anticipate and shape it."[12] Thus, whenever an "agency sends up a budget request it makes certain that there will be projects in it that will serve the districts represented by the members of the appropriations subcommittees as well as members of certain key legislative committees," adding "between 10 and 30 percent to the cost of the programs."[13]

For decades now, the incumbent-dominated Congress has cloaked big government in two main ways: debt financing and proxy administration. It has used debt financing to spare the public from having to pay for all the public benefits that it receives; otherwise, people would feel ever-bigger government digging ever deeper into their pockets. And it has used proxy administration to spare the public from reckoning with the federal government's ever-increasing size and scope; otherwise, citizens would come face-to-face with big government in the form of ever-bigger federal bureaucracies. As Martha Derthick has observed:

> Congress has habitually chosen the medium of grants not so much because it loves the states more as because it loves the federal bureaucracy less. Congress loves action—it thrives on policy proclamation and goal setting—but it hates bureaucracy and taxes, which are the instruments of action. Overwhelmingly, it has resolved this dilemma by turning over the bulk of administration to the state governments or any organizational instrumentality it can lay its hands on whose employees are not counted on the federal payroll.[14]

The federal judiciary is second only to Congress in shaping and sustaining Leviathan by Proxy. Whereas once the federal courts acted to restrain the national government's growth and hem in its authority, post-1960 federal judges have done far more to expand Washington's growth, to extend federal bureaucrats' authority, and to interpret federal laws and regulations in expansive ways whenever threats to the bureaucrats' delegated lawmaking authority have arisen.

By the early 1960s and the Great Society's dawn, Congress was already perfecting the faction-pleasing legislative process that is still with us today: reelection-minded incumbent congresspersons in both parties give diverse and even opposing interest groups much or all of what they want (for instance, business gets what it wants, but labor gets what it wants, too) and then delegate to federal bureaucrats broad authority to interpret federal law, translate it into administrative rules, fashion program features, set budget priorities, and deliver benefits.

Writing in 1969, Theodore J. Lowi lamented the "interest-group liberalism" that had come to define Washington's policymaking process.[15] Lowi stressed how New Deal–era federal judges had paved the way for the development not so much by what they did as by what they did not do: namely, uphold traditional constitutional prohibitions against delegating lawmaking powers to administrative agencies. For instance, in 1935, in *A.L.A. Schechter Poultry Corporation v. United States*, the U.S. Supreme Court declared that the National Industrial Recovery Act had gone too far in delegating legislative powers to appointed, not elected, officials. But, as Lowi noted, the "*Schechter* rule" had not been "seriously applied" since 1936.[16]

Today, four decades after Lowi called in vain for "restoration of the *Schechter* rule,"[17] and more than seven decades since its last serious application, the federal judiciary has done almost nothing to curb Congress's routine delegation of sweeping lawmaking powers to administrative agencies. Instead, it has created a now-settled body of federal law that authorizes delegation in areas ranging from environmental protection to defense procurement, homeland security to health care finance, and human services to education.

Indeed, over the last half-century, with the partial exception of federal grants to certain types of faith-based organizations, federal judges have only rarely pumped the brakes on *re*delegation of the federal bureaucrats' delegated lawmaking powers. This has led to unlimited Leviathan by Proxy: congresspersons in committees and subcommittees delegate to federal bureaucrats; federal bureaucrats delegate to other federal bureaucrats, to state and local government bureaucrats, to for-profit contractors, and to nonprofit grantees; and each proxy delegates to still other proxies (the federal grant-receiving state government agency delegates to other state government agencies and/or to multiple local government agencies and/or to multiple nongovernmental organizations, the for-profit contractors delegate to subcontractors, and so forth).

Many conservatives insist that liberal Democrats, left-wing causes, and powerful lefty interest groups like labor unions are behind both the "judicial activism" that accelerated government's growth and the legislative politics that spawned one new big government program after another. But the political right is only half right. For instance, from 1998 to 2012, the U.S. Chamber of Commerce spent nearly $1 billion lobbying federal policymakers.[18] The next biggest spenders were also pro-GOP business interests. Business lobbyists now outnumber lobbyists for labor unions and other liberal causes by 16 to 1, up from 12 to 1 in 1986.[19]

Moreover, before Obama, the largest continuous expansions in federal spending, programs, and powers actually occurred after Republicans regained the House in 1994 following forty years as the chamber's minority party. The expansions actually accelerated during the six years (2001–2007) when the GOP led both the House and the White House: Medicare exploded, defense and education spending increased, a new department formed, and the list goes on.

Leviathan by Proxy is ideologically androgynous and has a bipartisan pedigree. Thus, while Washington now has roughly the same number of full-time federal bureaucrats as it had in the early 1960s, it also pays millions more people—state and local government workers, for-profit contractors, nonprofit grantees—to administer its policies, programs, and regulations.

But the relationship between federal bureaucrats and proxies is rarely simple. For the most part, federal bureaucrats use their authority and discretion to fashion detailed administrative rules that limit the authority and discretion of the proxies. And Congress requires and the courts decree that federal bureaucrats do just that. But why?

The answer is that while Americans both love efficiency and loathe corruption, in its legislating and administrative oversight, Congress routinely emphasizes preventing corruption over achieving efficiency. Nobody knows, or blames Congress, when given federal programs fail to achieve efficiency gains, but everybody hears, and starts pointing fingers, when given federal programs suffer procurement scandals or the like. In both the court of public opinion and in courts of law, the best defense for both elected and appointed officials when such things happen is, in effect, to blame the proxies for not doing their jobs or "following the rules."

The proxies know this too, and their seemingly ironic but perfectly rational, practical, and self-protective response is to request ever more detailed grants and contracts, ever more precise reporting requirements, and so forth (even as they complain about "federal bureaucracy" and "too much paperwork"). Federal bureaucrats are quick to oblige them. Thus, over time, the system becomes ever more rule-bound, ever more liability-managed, and, hence, ever less about performance, results, cost-effectiveness, and efficiency gains. The grantees or contractors, the agencies, and the congressional oversight committees each find a refuge in red tape.

Writing in 1967, James Q. Wilson smelled this "bureaucracy problem"[20] brewing. Congress was becoming ever more prone to enact long and convoluted laws that embodied multiple, vague, and contradictory objectives. Such laws would be increasingly difficult for federal agencies to administer wisely or well. Public spirited or not, competent or not, federal bureaucrats would be able to achieve efficiency gains with respect to given legislatively mandated goals only at the expense of disregarding or discounting other legislatively mandated goals.

Today, Congress routinely enacts sprawling, supersized laws that only federal bureaucrats read closely from cover to cover. Federal bureaucrats then translate them into action by, in effect, telling themselves and their proxies what to do and what to spend by way of administering it. Keep in mind, in most years since 1965, Congress has enacted more than 200 new laws. In all but six years since 1965, Congress has enacted no fewer than 150 new laws, including sixteen years when it enacted 300 or more. Even with the recent nosedive in Congress's legislative productivity (a total of fewer than 300 new laws were enacted from 2011 through 2013), since 1999, Congress has enacted about 2,500 new laws plus tens of thousands of new law-related rules and regulations.

Leading political scientists, including Wilson and Lowi, have crafted useful taxonomies of the federal policymaking process,[21] and other political scientists, notably John Kingdon and Nelson Polsby, have developed various frameworks for understanding federal agenda setting and policy innovation.[22] For the most part, however, most average citizens, academics, activists, and journalists divide federal laws into different policy domains. We think about tax policy, education policy, environmental policy, health policy, defense policy, and so on. That's fine, too, so far as it goes.

But a better way to understand how big government in America really works is to recognize that most federal laws, in whichever policy domain, authorize Washington to do one or more of four main things: (1) pay subsidies to particular groups and organizations in society, (2) transfer money to state and local governments, (3) award grants or contracts to for-profit firms and nonprofit organizations, and (4) devise and enforce regulations on the society and the economy. (Think STAR: subsidies, transfers, awards, and regulations.)

President Abraham Lincoln spoke of our representative democracy as "government of the people, by the people, for the people." But today's Leviathan by Proxy is government of the people-placating incumbents, by the outsourcing bureaucrats, for the entrenched interest groups. It now spends about $6 trillion a year and will spend more than $7 trillion a year before 2020, borrowing hundreds of billions of dollars a year along the way. It pays millions of state and local government employees, for-profit contractors, and nonprofit grantees as de facto federal government administrators. It pays millions more private citizens as federal or federal-state program beneficiaries.

Leviathan by Proxy is a uniquely American, superficially antistatist form of big government that has entered into every nook and cranny of both public and private life. If you doubt it, just try to name ten adult U.S. citizens you know who have never received any federal, state, local, or intergovernmental government payments, loans, subsidies, grants, contracts, or other benefits whatsoever. (OK, can you name just five?) Or just try to identify any activity in which you engage; any space that you traverse; any building that you enter (including your own private home); any product or service that you produce, buy, or sell (including private health insurance); or, for that matter, any air that you breathe on which there is no government policy, program, or regulation. (Give up?)

Big government in drag dressed as state or local government, private enterprise, or civil society is still big government. Growth in this American "state" is harder to restrain, and its performance ills are harder to diagnose and cure, than they would be in a big government more directly administered by federal bureaucrats.

For instance, the American Recovery and Reinvestment Act (ARRA) of 2009 was a roughly $800 billion "stimulus bill." Whatever its impact on the nation's economy, ARRA definitely stimulated many federal proxies. By 2013, twenty-eight federal agencies disbursed ARRA money and ARRA had accounted for about $290 billion in federal tax benefits, $250 billion in federal entitlement payments, and another $250 billion in more than 80,000 federal grants, contracts, or loans to state and local governments, for-profit businesses, and nonprofit organizations.[23] Many ARRA proxies received both grants and contracts, functioning as "primary recipients" on some awards, "subrecipients" on others, and "vendors" on still others.

To their great credit, the Obama administration and concerned congressional leaders in both parties saw to it that ARRA was flanked by new or enhanced financial reporting requirements. And thanks to dedicated federal civil servants (including inspectors general), most ARRA grant-making federal agencies made good-faith efforts to follow ARRA money and measure its "recovery and reinvestment" results.

Still, with so much additional money flowing to so many proxies (and proxies' proxies), ARRA grants and contracts were not always managed and monitored terribly well. The Department of Health and Human Services (HHS) alone dispensed more than 35,000 ARRA grants and 5,000 ARRA contracts while remaining responsible for both the Medicare program and the Medicaid program. Together, Medicare and Medicaid account for about a fifth of the federal budget. Each program has more than 50 million beneficiaries, each is in financial trouble, each is growing rapidly, each has experienced major "improper payments" scandals, and each is "run" by a tiny HHS unit, the Centers for Medicare and Medicaid Services (CMS), which has fewer than 5,000 full-time employees.

As Donald F. Kettl has observed, Washington "does not so much run" Medicare and Medicaid "as leverage them."[24] When Kettl's own late mother-in-law, Mildred, ended up in a nursing home with multiple medical maladies, Medicare and Medicaid paid her bills. During the two years before Mildred died, she saw or spoke to doctors, nurses, ambulance drivers, pharmacists, health aids, hospital administrators, bill-processing agents, and myriad other persons; but "*she never met a single government employee. Not one.*"[25]

As Kettl further chronicled, "throughout her care—whose taxpayer-borne costs totaled hundreds of thousands of dollars—no one was in charge."[26] Mildred's Medicare and Medicaid experience typified the "paradox of government service payment without government service provision" and its "corollary of government spending without government control of the decisions that shape the costs and the quality" of the care and services supplied.[27]

Echoing Mildred's saga, in the November 2013 *AARP Bulletin*, the featured story about Medicare began with this frequently asked question: "As a government-run system, will Medicare give me inferior care?" The story's spot-on answer:

> No. . . . The federal government runs and regulates Medicare, and also pays around 75 percent of the cost of the medical services you use. Even so, those actual services are almost wholly private. The doctors you go to are not government employees; the hospitals and laboratories that provide services to you are not government-owned. Instead, they're free to enter (or not enter) into contracts with Medicare as they choose.[28]

The AARP story ended by reassuring new Medicare beneficiaries that Obamacare would, if anything, simply increase
their proxy-provided benefits over time:

> The Affordable Care Act guarantees all current
> Medicare beneficiaries and provides more. It makes
> many preventive services, such as mammograms,
> free of charge, and slashes the cost of prescription
> drugs.[29]

Obamacare is not a road to a European-style, single-payer
health care system, and America does not have "socialized
medicine." But America has long had a big government
health care finance system just the same. In 2000, health care
spending in the United States was about 13.7 percent of GDP
compared to an average of 7.8 percent of GDP for Britain,
France, Germany, and the rest of the thirty-four Organization for Economic Co-operation and Development (OECD)
nations.[30] By 2011, health care spending in the United States
had risen to 17.7 percent of GDP compared to an average of
9.3 percent of GDP for all OECD nations.[31]

In various reports issued in 2014, the CMS noted that the
rate of increase in U.S. health care spending had slowed.[32]
It had, but a slower "rate of increase" is not a decrease—
besides, since 2009, health care spending growth has leveled
off in most OECD nations. The OECD reported that the
"drop has been primarily driven by a collapse in the growth
of government health spending."[33] But America's Leviathan

by Proxy is still spending, and will continue to spend, more on both Medicare and Medicaid, among other big government health care finance programs.

Blame Hillary Clinton or Barack Obama if you want, but when America's big government health care finance system began, she had just campaigned for Barry Goldwater and he was only four years old. Medicare and Medicaid became law in 1965. Ever since then, America has had a Washington-leveraged, administratively ramshackle, but ever-growing big government health care finance system. As the AARP advised, Obamacare simply "provides more."[34]

Ah, but now America's Leviathan by Proxy health care finance system has six different species of "health exchanges" (federal, state, and federal-state, some expanding the federal-state Medicaid program, some not) and features (and funds) literally thousands more for-profit and nonprofit prox-ies (including "navigators"). And now, beyond the much-publicized information technology and other administrative bungles that plagued Obamacare's early implementation, there are myriad new intergovernmental health care policy implementation messes on the horizon, and they are likely to persist for many years to come.

In 2013, while still maintaining responsibility for the mammoth Medicare and Medicaid program duo, CMS was also supposed to oversee Obamacare's implementation in all fifty states, set up "health exchanges" in the thirty-six states that opted to let Washington take the lead in shouldering that chore, and gather in new legions of nongovernmental contractors and grantees. What's amazing is that it worked at all.

For a half-century now, Washington policymakers in both parties have grown big government by passing far-reaching federal laws that reflect not the slightest real regard for what it takes to translate the policies, programs, or regulations into timely and cost-effective administrative action. (Ensuring that enough presidential souvenir pens are ready for distribution to key congressional cosponsors at bill-signing ceremonies at the White House Rose Garden does not count.) Consider, for example, how they brought Leviathan by Proxy to environmental protection.

Until the mid-twentieth century, environmental protection was hardly a blip on the federal government's agenda. Among the early federal environmental protection laws were the National Environmental Protection Act, the Clean Air Act, the Clean Water Act, the Toxic Substances Control Act, and the Resource Conservation and Recovery Act. The first Earth Day was in 1970. That same year, the Environmental Protection Agency (EPA) was established. But the first major surge to Leviathan by Proxy on environmental protection came a decade later when Congress passed and President Jimmy Carter signed the Comprehensive Environmental Response, Compensation, and Liability Act (CERCLA) of 1980.

CERCLA created the Superfund program. Then as now, Superfund was dedicated mainly to cleaning up the nation's toxic or hazardous waste sites. Since starting Superfund,

Congress has tasked the EPA with responsibility for dozens more environmental policies, programs, and regulations, including, in recent years, new initiatives to combat global warming. Today, the United States has what is arguably the largest and most complicated body of environmental protection laws in the world.

In 1980, at Superfund's start, the EPA had about 13,000 full-time staff.[35] Decade by decade, Congress radically expanded the EPA's mission and responsibilities, but there was no commensurate increase in the EPA's staff. Rather, Congress set and maintained annual ceilings on the number of staff that work the equivalent of a full year for the EPA.[36]

In fact, the EPA's staff ceiling was lowered from 18,000 positions in 2001 to about 17,000 in 2012.[37] As the Government Accountability Office (GAO) has noted, "EPA relies extensively on states, public and private entities, and other federal agencies to implement most environmental programs by awarding grants and contracts."[38] For example, in 2010, the EPA sent about $4.5 billion to state agencies, awarded contracts—including several for $50 million or more—to for-profit businesses, granted nearly a quarter-billion dollars to nonprofit organizations, and made other awards and "subawards."[39]

State governments have been, and continue to be, the EPA's primary proxies, and many larger urban municipalities have some "environment and energy" contingent within city government and a "Green Power Partnership" with the EPA.[40]

The Environmental Council for the States has estimated that by 2007 about 96 percent of all EPA programs (up from 40 percent in 1992) were administered by state agencies that employed thousands of environmental protection workers:

> State environmental agencies are responsible for implementing nearly all of the core environmental programs.... Most of the major federal environmental statutes are designed for states to assume authority over the federal programs under the oversight of the Environmental Protection Agency.[41]

Meanwhile, the EPA's private contractors have answered its hotlines, advised businesses about which projects might be eligible for government funding, and even developed the EPA's own official criteria for deciding which program functions it ought not to administer by proxies.[42] And the EPA's nonprofit grantees, including tax-exempt think tank analysts and university researchers, have often led in "educating" Congress about the need for more EPA-leveraged federal policies, programs, or regulations. As Gerald J. Garvey has described it:

> Governance in environmental policy is a major industry, not just a handful of programs. The federal-state-local regime evolved erratically through continuous political negotiation and technical refinement,

always with insistent involvement by industry lobbyists and technicians and by representatives of environmental protection groups.[43]

Compared to the environmental protection regimes of
many European democracies, America's Leviathan by Proxy
environmental protection regime has been more adversarial
when it comes to enforcing regulations on both individuals
and organizations. For example, as David Vogel has shown,
in the United Kingdom, government and business leaders acting cooperatively wrote far-reaching rules designed to reduce
air pollution.[44] The rules were neither rigid nor uniform.
Compliance with the rules depended mostly on voluntary
action. Lawsuits were rare.

Today, more than four decades after the EPA was established and more than three decades after CERCLA was
enacted, it is still the case that one in four Americans lives
within three miles of a hazardous waste site.[45] The EPA is
spread across ten administrative regions, and about 2,000
of its some 3,400 national priority cleanup sites are handled
"outside the Superfund program."[46] In many places, "the
cleanup is conducted by a private party."[47] But because the
data on all the EPA's assorted Superfund proxies remain so
spotty, it is "impossible to determine the exact number of
sites that EPA oversees under the Superfund program that are
not being addressed," and "there is no consistently applied
method for tracking them."[48]

Such decades-old policy implementation problems plague many less visible but quite important EPA programs, too. For example, today in the United States more than 16,000 pesticides—chemical or biological substances that kill or control weeds, insects, and more—are in use.[49] There are GAO reports stretching back to 1980 regarding problems with the EPA's pesticide registration process. In 2013, there were just twenty EPA Office of Pesticide Programs (OPP) managers. Each OPP manager was responsible for tracking about eight hundred "active pesticide registrations."[50] Many OPP managers have relied on "reminder notices, handwritten notes, and memory" to "track down the status of pesticide registrations."[51] Thus, the EPA has doled out "conditional registrations" for new pesticides in ways that could compromise its capacity to catch and quickly correct any adverse "public health and environmental impacts caused by pesticides."[52]

Environmental protection issues like global warming divide Democrats and Republicans,[53] but nearly everyone is for supplying public benefits to the nation's more than 27 million military veterans and their families. In 1930, three separate federal agencies were consolidated into the Veterans Administration. That administration was succeeded in 1989 by the cabinet-level department that has since grown to about 300,000 civilian employees.

Today's Department of Veterans Affairs, widely known simply as the VA, boasts "the largest integrated health system in America," encompassing 151 hospitals and 827 community-based outpatient clinics.[54] Each year, the VA processes nearly 1 million claims for disability benefits, and its fifty-three regional offices also oversee some 6.8 million life insurance policies, 131 national cemeteries, and more.[55]

Second only to the Department of Defense (DOD) in the size of its full-time workforce, the VA, like the DOD, is still highly dependent on contractors. Here's how the VA's Office of Acquisition and Logistics opens its statement on "Doing Business with VA":

> The mission of the Department of Veterans Affairs is one of service to more than 27 million veterans who have so unselfishly served their country. To accomplish this mission, the products and services of industry are required by a nationwide system of hospitals, clinics, Veterans Integrated Service Networks (VISN), data processing centers, and National Cemeteries which require a broad spectrum of goods and services. . . . So no matter how large or small your business is, VA is a potential customer.[56]

And here is a VA-related excerpt from the *Federal and Foundation Assistance Monitor* issued on October 25, 2013, just after the federal government shutdown ended:

> With the federal government once again open for business, lawmakers are scurrying to finalize spend-

ing plans for Fiscal Year 2014—and high on the list of top priorities is funding for veterans' programs. Join us (for) . . . a 75-minute, information-packed audio conference designed to give grant-seekers the competitive edge they need to obtain funding for programs aimed at helping veterans. . . . Participants in this unique, upcoming audio conference will learn where to find federal and private funding resources. . . . It's the kind of information you'll use again and again.[57]

A Contract Officer's Representatives (COR) workforce oversees the performance of contractors at VA medical centers. Most of the 40 CORs across four VA medical centers studied by the GAO had "other primary responsibilities, such as serving as a business manager or administrative officer for a specialty clinic within" the VA medical center.[58] On average, each COR spent only about a quarter of his or her time monitoring an average of a dozen contracts. The GAO concluded that the CORs "lack tools, such as standard templates, that should be included in common types of clinical contracts. . . . Without a robust monitoring system, VA cannot ensure that" VA medical centers "are properly monitoring, evaluating, and documenting the performance of contract providers caring for veterans."[59]

In sum, America has not had limited government for at least a half-century now. Rather, it has had a Washington–

leveraged big government. Leviathan by Proxy is expensive and expansive. It is unduly influenced by special interests that function as federal proxies. And it is now increasingly prone to costly and colossal administrative failures.

Leviathan by Proxy's defining administrative dysfunction is not simply that there are never enough full-time federal bureaucrats around when you need them, such as to coordinate medical care at hospitals for veterans or to clean up toxic waste sites. Rather, Leviathan by Proxy's defining administrative dysfunction is that the federal civil servants, who often are too few to do the work themselves, are also too few, too inexperienced, or too poorly trained and equipped to meaningfully manage and monitor the proxies that do the work instead.

CHAPTER 3

The Federal Workforce Is Overloaded, Not Bloated

$\geq\leq$

THE HARD TRUTHS regarding how much big government America actually has and how deeply dysfunctional America's big government has become are nobody's favorite civics lesson or stump speech. Indeed, in his January 1996 State of the Union address, President Bill Clinton boldly proclaimed that the "era of big government is over," and in August 1996, he declared that Washington was on the way to "ending welfare as we know it."

It is true that during the 1990s, after expanding almost nonstop for three decades, federal government spending slowed, a few federal budget surpluses were recorded, and a means-tested federal-state welfare program, Aid to Families with Dependent Children, was abolished. But, in the 2000s, federal spending resumed its post-1960 growth. By 2012, successive trillion-dollar budget deficits had been recorded. The abolished Aid to Families with Dependent Children was just one of several dozen antipoverty programs and was by no means the biggest. It never accounted for as much as 1 percent of the federal budget. Besides, it was immediately replaced by another federal-state welfare program, Temporary Assistance to Needy Families.

President Clinton and Vice President Al Gore did, however, push to improve big government's performance. In the 1990s, the Clinton-Gore National Performance Review (NPR) followed four other major federal bureaucracy reform efforts: the Eisenhower-Kennedy-Johnson presidential study commissions on executive reorganization (1953–68), the Nixon-backed Ash Council (1969–71), the Carter federal government reorganization initiative (1977–79), and the Reagan-backed Grace Commission (1982–84). Taken together, these efforts aimed to improve government purchasing practices, streamline agency budgets, recruit or retain better full-time civil service workers, and contain wasteful or duplicative spending. Each effort bore some fruit, most notably, perhaps, the federal procurement process reforms that resulted from the NPR and expanded somewhat under both the G. W. Bush administration and the Obama administration.

Still, as has been documented in study after study over the last several decades, the "federal government faces significant and long-standing fiscal, management, and performance challenges."[1] In several studies, the Government Accountability Office (GAO) has documented more than one hundred areas of federal government duplication, overlap, fragmentation, and foregone cost-savings.[2] Many attempts to fix these problems have been hamstrung or halted by "the absence of a comprehensive list of federal programs" and "the lack of related funding information."[3]

You read that right: official Washington is officially unable to so much as name all the programs that it authorizes, let alone to describe exactly how the programs are administered or to track closely all the tax money that it doles out for programs.

The federal government does not have complete and reliable information regarding what agencies are responsible for which programs.[4] The reason is not just the (literally untold) number of federal programs, but the fact that many federal programs are administered, and "tens of billions of dollars" are spent annually, via three different types of "interagency contract vehicles" that are so fraught with problems ("awarding out-of-scope work and not complying with laws and regulations") that the "use of interagency contracts" has been on the GAO's "government-wide high risk" list for nearly a decade now.[5]

Beyond the federal bureaucracy's own internal, maze-like administrative and financial gymnastics, there are the cascading complications attendant to keeping close tabs on what (often multiple) federal agencies or (often multiple) subagency units spend and do via myriad state and local government agencies, for-profit firms, and nonprofit organizations. For instance, even in relatively small-budget federal policy domains like, say, federal child welfare programs, how states "spend and blend" federal funds and administer federal programs can vary tremendously and defy easy program categorization, tracking, and performance assessment.[6]

Moreover, many a federal or federal-state program's "implementation chain" is not only long but is linked to twisted strands of nongovernmental program proxies (for-profit contractors, nonprofit grantees, or both) and nongovernmental proxies' proxies (subcontractors, subgrantees, or both). Thus, for more than a few federal programs, there is no "comprehensive estimate" of "the amount of federal grant funds awarded from prime recipients to subrecipients."[7]

It should come as no surprise, therefore, that neither the Government Performance and Results Act of 1993 nor the Government Performance and Results Modernization Act of 2010 have been well or fully implemented. Today, federal managers are no more likely to use "information on performance measurement when coordinating program efforts with other internal or external organizations" than they were in 1997. Nearly a quarter of the federal managers surveyed in 2013 "reported that they coordinated program efforts to a small extent or not at all."[8]

The inconvenient truth is that the federal workforce has shrunk, not only relative to how much money rushes through it, but also relative to the number and complexity of the tasks that it is supposed to execute, the interagency partnerships it is supposed to maintain, and the proxies that it is supposed to manage and monitor.

Consider, for example, the Federal Emergency Management Agency (FEMA). FEMA's response to Hurricane Katrina in 2005, and its role in the post-Katrina human, physical, and financial recovery process, has been harshly criticized, and rightly so. But many critics have failed to notice that the FEMA that failed so spectacularly in the Gulf Coast had in the preceding half decade become home to a downsized, inexperienced, and overloaded federal workforce.

FEMA "operates somewhat like a volunteer fire department" with a workforce that is mostly "composed of non-permanent employees with various terms."[9] In the years just before Katrina, the Department of Homeland Security (DHS) subsumed FEMA and the agency "experienced near-constant organizational change."[10] Pre-DHS, FEMA's vast and varied responsibilities included "off-site consequences of accidents at nuclear power plants, hazardous waste materials emergency management, chemical weapons disposal," and more.[11] Between 2001 and 2005, Congress gave FEMA about $1.5 billion in new programs to administer, and the DHS added "acts of terrorism" plus "other man-made disasters" to the agency's duty roster.[12]

As FEMA's responsibilities changed and grew, it lost a quarter of its most experienced senior management employees. In 2004, the year before Katrina, the agency was subject to a congressionally sanctioned hiring freeze on more than five hundred open positions. Thus, the FEMA that responded so poorly to Katrina had already been acutely short-staffed for nearly a half decade; it could not easily "run existing programs" let alone avoid "delays in implementing new programs."[13] When Katrina hit, FEMA had about 2,100 full-time positions; it also had inexperienced people in many top management positions.[14]

In recent years, however, a new and better chapter in FEMA's history has begun.[15] With the White House and DHS leadership eager to avoid more blame, and with congresspersons on the relevant "administrative oversight" committees forced to pay closer attention, FEMA was authorized to add full-time staff and give extra resources to retain its most experienced remaining senior managers. Between 2007 and 2012, there were some 422 major federal disaster declarations, and FEMA obligated $39 billion in disaster assistance or relief payments.[16] In 2012, FEMA's response to Hurricane Sandy was not perfect, but it was near perfect by comparison to its Katrina follies. When Sandy hit, FEMA had about 4,800 full-time positions, or more than double the number that it had when Katrina hit.

Even now, FEMA, which depends on more than 6,700 "reservists" to bolster its "disaster workforce," needs to "improve its reservist training efforts" and get a firmer handle on its contractor workforce.[17] Still, all things considered, FEMA has improved, and its federal workforce challenges seem manageable compared to those now faced by many other federal agencies.

For instance, today's Social Security Administration (SSA) is experiencing acute organizational problems much like those that weakened FEMA in the early 2000s. The SSA administers three main programs: Old Age and Survivors Insurance (OASI), Disability Insurance (DI), and Supplemental Security Income (SSI). The SSA pays for states' Disability Determination Services (DDS) agencies. The SSA has more than 80,000 state (DDS and other) and federal employees in about 1,700 facilities nationwide (regional offices, field offices, processing centers, hearings offices, Appeals Council, and more).[18] Each day, about 180,000 people visit SSA offices in person, and more than 450,000 call SSA offices.[19] In 2012, the SSA's programs had 62 million beneficiaries that received some $826 billion.[20]

By 2025, the SSA's beneficiary population will exceed 85 million people and the agency will disburse nearly $1.8 trillion.[21] But the SSA "projects that it could lose nearly 22,500 employees, or nearly one-third of its workforce," by 2020, which is when some 7,000 SSA headquarters employees and 24,000 SSA field employees become eligible for retirement.[22] In recent years, due to a congressionally mandated hiring freeze, the SSA has been unable to "back-fill positions vacated by retiring employees."[23]

Thus, the SSA's workload is increasing, but its workforce is decreasing. It is clear that "without a sufficient number of skilled employees, backlogs and wait times could significantly increase and improper payments could grow."[24] The short-staffed SSA has already experienced security breakdowns in its "computer systems and networks."[25] You need not be a human resources expert or a personnel management guru to guess why "low morale and a feeling of being stretched too thin are hastening retirement among those who are eligible."[26] The SSA "risks losing institutional knowledge and expertise at a time when workloads and service demands are increasing."[27]

The SSA is popular with both politicians and the public, and FEMA's core mission—helping mange emergencies— is valued even when the agency is vilified. Not so with the Internal Revenue Service (IRS). In part for that reason, for more than two decades now, Congress and successive presidents have ignored report after report documenting how the IRS's workforce was gradually imploding beneath the weight of nonstop increases in its workload. For instance, in 2002, Charles O. Rossotti, then IRS Commissioner, candidly assessed the agency's 1992 to 2002 staffing shortages:

> Over the last ten years, the size and complexity of the tax system increased enormously. Beyond the simple increase in the number of taxpayers and revenue dollars, the majority of tax dollars now come from sources that are more subject to manipulation by those who wish to pay less than the law requires and much more difficult and time consuming for our agents to uncover. Meanwhile, the size of the IRS declined, not just relatively but in absolute terms, because of budget constraints . . . creating a major gap in IRS capacity to manage the tax system.[28]

Between 1992 and 2001, the IRS lost 16 percent of its full-time workforce and major administrative problems erupted; but, for the most part, calls to bolster the agency's "human capital" were either ignored or lampooned on Capitol Hill.[29] Nothing much changed in the 2000s. In 2011 and 2012, the IRS lost about 10,000 more full-time employees; it began 2013 with about 90,000 positions.[30] A 2013 report by the Treasury Inspector General for Tax Administration stressed that many among the IRS's "most experienced leaders and employees will be eligible to retire in the next five years," making it harder for the agency to "implement significant tax code changes" and "stop billions of dollars in fraudulent or improper tax refunds resulting from identity theft and erroneous claims for tax credits."[31]

For several decades now, billions of dollars owed in federal taxes have gone uncollected each year. This tax gap problem has grown worse as the IRS has become ever more short-staffed both in absolute terms and relative to the size and complexity of its duties.

For instance, the IRS estimated that the tax gap in 1973 was about $31 billion, or, in constant 2006 dollars, about $136 billion.[32] In 2006, the tax gap was about $450 billion, more than triple what it was in 1973.[33]

The silver lining here is that, even as its workforce sags, the IRS recovers significant tax gap dollars. For instance, for 2006, through various enforcement efforts and audits, the agency eventually recovered around $65 billion of the $450 billion that was owed but unpaid.[34] That left a net tax gap of $385 billion for 2006. And most IRS recovery efforts are highly cost-effective. For instance, for every dollar that the IRS spends on "correspondence exams" involving taxpayers reporting annual incomes between $220,000 and $1 million, the agency recovers about $25.[35]

Still, put the 1973 to 2013 federal tax gap in constant 2013 dollars, and conservatively estimate the average annual net tax gap at $150 billion and the total forty-year tax gap at $6 trillion. In other words, the total tax gap for that period would be about enough to fund the entire federal government *and* all state and local governments in 2014—or enough to pay down (or never incur in the first place) about 35 percent of the now roughly $17 trillion national debt.

Short-staffing the IRS must take the prize as the last half-century's single most pennywise but pound-foolish federal workforce policy. For, even if it would have taken more than double the IRS workforce total (say a 200,000-agent IRS with each employee costing, in today's dollars, $150,000 a year for the entire forty-year period) to recover just a fifth of that $150 billion a year tax gap (or $30 billion a year), the workforce expansion would have paid for itself ($30 billion a year more collected, $30 billion a year for the workforce).

Counterfactual history and what-if calculations aside, today's IRS has fewer than 5,000 employees in its investigations unit. The agency's staff is stretched too thin to do more than a perfunctory job of overseeing organizations that are tax-exempt under section 501(c)(3) of the federal tax code.

Since the mid-1980s, as the IRS workforce has remained flat or fallen, the number of nonprofit organizations has increased about fivefold to more than 1.6 million. In 2012, in just one nonprofit subsector—human services—some 200,000 government grants and contracts went to about 30,000 nonprofit organizations.[36] Even if the IRS devoted all of its oversight resources to just the sliver of the nonprofit sector comprised of groups receiving government grants or contracts, each IRS civil servant would have more than enough work to do.

But rather than expand the IRS's workforce so as to expand the agency's highly cost-effective tax gap recovery programs, in the mid-2000s, Congress opted instead to outsource tax collections to private contractors. The proxy tax collection push began in 2006. By 2009, predictable problems with protecting taxpayer data privacy, allegations concerning contractors using high-pressure tactics, contractor noncompliance with IRS rules, and other concerns brought this initiative to a close.

Contracted, *Not* Privatized

Unfortunately, far worse federal contracting arrangements, many of them decades old, are everywhere one looks in the federal bureaucracy. In Leviathan by Proxy, whatever the federal-law-mandated task—collecting taxes, disbursing disability checks, managing natural or man-made disasters and emergencies, getting good buys on military weapons systems, getting good buys on mass transit equipment, curbing financial fraud in health care, securing federal facilities that handle plutonium, or whatever—severe and persistent "performance and results" problems plague the federal bureaucracy's contracting process and what in fed-speak is known as Washington's "acquisition workforce."

To oversimplify a bit, the federal contracting process has three separate but related parts: (1) planning (how federal agencies decide what and how much to contract for, when they need given goods or services to be delivered, and what terms and conditions are they subject to); (2) awarding (the background market research, the communications and outreach to prospective contractors, the budgetary criteria, and the precise procedures for awarding competitive bids or making noncompetitive selections); and (3) overseeing (everything from routine reporting requirements to financial audits, field inspections, public comments, and impact studies).

The Department of Defense (DOD) contracts out more than any other agency. The DOD "has increasingly relied on contractors both overseas and in the United States to perform many of the same functions as civilian employees," including management support, communication services, interpreters, weapons system maintenance, and more.[37]

But even at the gargantuan DOD, with its more than 700,000 full-time contractor positions and more than $300 billion a year in contracts, the acquisition workforce has long been undertrained and short-staffed. For instance, when the Pentagon awarded contracts for the $385 billion F-35 weapons program—contracts to build the ultimate stealth plane—all three parts of the contracting process broke down in ways that resulted in years of huge cost overruns, engineering design changes by the thousands, repeated slowdowns in production, and a nearly 20 percent decrease in the number of planes ultimately developed and delivered.[38]

There is, however, nothing inevitable about such Grand Canyon–sized snags in federal contracting. For instance, between 2010 and 2013, when the DOD not only added about 3,500 personnel to its acquisition workforce but also trained them better than usual for the job, the agency's on-time contract compliance assessments increased by nearly a third.[39]

Each federal agency, even relatively small ones, has its acquisition workforce too; but smaller is by no means automatically better. For instance, the Department of Energy (DOE), with a core staff of about 15,000 full-time federal workers, spends 90 percent of a roughly $30 billion annual budget on contracts, including twenty contractors that in 2013 each received between $250 million and $3.7 billion.[40] As the DOE states on its energy.gov website, "staff and contractors are the heart of everything" the agency does.[41]

But that heart has a dangerous administrative murmur. For example, when it comes to managing contractors and monitoring operations like those subsumed by its Plutonium Disposition Program, there are "numerous, long-standing, and systemic security issues across the nuclear security enterprise, and significant problems remain at DOE sites that have not been fully addressed."[42] The problems include "lax attitudes toward safety procedures" and "inadequate oversight"; and, for "more than a decade," the DOE has not maintained data sufficient to "identify the costs of its activities and ensure the validity of its cost estimates."[43]

Even smaller than DOE, the Department of Transportation (DOT) spends about $5.5 billion on contracting. The DOT has eleven Operating Administrations (OA) units. Five OA units together spent 90 percent of the agency's procurement dollars.[44] In 2013, they lacked "sufficient numbers of adequately trained acquisition professionals" and four of the five OA units "needed to replace 50 percent or more of their contract specialists" within the year or face "substantial risks that the workforce will not have the capacity or skills needed to effectively manage the department's acquisitions."[45]

But perhaps the worst, or at least the most dispiriting, problems with Leviathan by Proxy's contracting process are those that involve ongoing fraud that is well documented and widely known but never corrected. For instance, each year, the Department of Health and Human Services and the Department of Justice spend more than half a billion dollars to combat and catch fraud and abuse in Medicare and Medicaid.[46] The good news is that the effort pays dividends: roughly $4.3 billion was recovered in 2012, or about $7.90 for every $1.00 spent.[47] But the bad news is that, in 2012, Medicare alone made an estimated $32.4 billion in "improper payments" that included contractors billing for supplies or services that they did not deliver, billing at higher rates than were allowed by law, or paying kickbacks for steering beneficiaries to particular practices or suppliers.[48]

Medicare has been on the Government Accountability Office's "high risk" list for twenty-three years. The Leviathan by Proxy history behind Medicare's antifraud program problems is instructive. Contractors "have a long-standing and essential role in the Medicare program" that extends to policing other contractors.[49] From 1965 through 1996, Congress expressly authorized that Medicare have two types of contractors, one known as "fiscal intermediaries," and the other known as "carriers." Thereafter, Congress authorized four types of contractors to conduct postpayment reviews on Medicare fee-for-service claims: Medicare Administrative Contractors, Zone Program Integrity Contractors, Recovery Auditors, and Comprehensive Error Rate Testing contractors. Each of the four was authorized under a separate law, and there are—to put it mildly—wide differences in postpayment review procedures. More than 1 billion Medicare claims are processed each year, but less than 1 percent of all Medicare claims are reviewed (this includes both automated and other techniques).[50] In 2002 and in 2010, Congress enacted an Improper Payments Act, but the laws have not reduced the need for "greater consistency in the claims review process across contractors"—and they certainly have not ended "improper payments."[51]

Back in the 1980s, thinking libertarians made a credible

case for "privatization"—that is, "the transfer of a function, in whole or in part, from the public sector to the private sector."[52] President Reagan's almost romantic proprivatization rhetoric was backed by many good empirical studies. For instance, E. S. Savas and others had found that for-profit businesses operating under relatively free market conditions performed many functions in a more cost-effective fashion than government agencies did: trash collection, street cleaning, ship maintenance, housing construction, school bus operation, railroad track repair, mental health services, day care, fire protection, K-12 schools, minimum-security prisons, and more.[53] Among the functions studied, the only two major exceptions to the "privatization works" thesis were electric utilities and hospitals.[54]

But Leviathan by Proxy's contracting out is not privatizing—it is privatization's antithesis:

- The government "market" often features poorly trained and short-staffed "acquisition workforce" bureaucrats using tax dollars to purchase goods and services for other people.
- The public procurement officials must please reelection-minded legislators and thus must "shop" subject to politically tinged legal constraints, not in accordance with "consumer preferences."
- The flaws of the contract process undermine the quality of goods and services. In the economic marketplace, if

you like a good or service at the price you paid for it, you become a repeat customer; if you don't like it or feel overcharged, you stop patronizing the supplier. But, until the Clinton-Gore "reinventing government" initiative, federal agencies behaved as if they were forbidden to take "vendor past performance" into account when awarding contracts.[55]

- The old methods of the contract process have persisted despite changes in federal rules. During the Clinton-Gore years, federal rules that discouraged procurement officials from taking contractors' past performance into account were reduced or repealed, but bureaucratic behavior reflecting the old, perverse protocols still lives on today "in the real world of government contracting."[56]
- The contracting process is often closer to being closed than it is to being competitive. In 2008, for example, two-thirds of all federal contracts and half of all federal contract dollars were awarded without "full and open competition."[57]
- The government awards hundreds of thousands of single-bidder contracts. In 2012, the DOD alone awarded more than 100,000 single-bidder contracts and task orders worth, all told, more than $150 billion,[58] much of it going to DOD-dependent "defense companies" that rely on Washington for most of their annual revenues.

The "competition" for government contracts is not only among for-profit businesses, but between them and nonprofit organizations. Yet the same top "awardees," both for-profit and nonprofit, dominate the process year after year. Nearly half of nonprofit organizations boast budgets that total $1 million a year or more (think everything from major private universities to religious megacharities to brand-name national antipoverty organizations), and more than a third of nonprofit organizations have both government grants and contracts.[59] Six-figure and seven-figure government and foundation grants are common funding fare among big-budget nonprofit organizations. Their board members and (often quite well-compensated) executive leaders know that while big government's grant money is never guaranteed, it is usually predictable and reliable enough to build into their multiyear budget plans.

By contrast, nonprofit organizations with annual budgets below $100,000 (think local religious congregations and other community-based groups) make up about 40 percent of the "reporting" organizations that register with the IRS.[60] Given the prevalence of religious congregations in the nonreporting ranks, most tax-exempt organizations spend less than six figures a year. These small-budget nonprofits, not least the urban, minority-led, religious congregations, supply myriad health and human services to scores of millions of people without regard to anyone's religion, yet few receive any government grants or contracts whatsoever.[61]

In the late 1990s and early 2000s, top leaders in both parties rallied around the case for expanding government funding for community-serving religious nonprofit organizations, including sacred places that served secular and civic purposes and did not discriminate on religious grounds in hiring.[62] But many large nonprofit organizations, both religious and secular, that had long been Washington's go-to grant recipients, coalesced into a strange-bedfellows coalition (some behind the scenes, but others in public) against federal "faith-based and community initiatives." Some, including religious megacharity leaders with organizations that had received millions of dollars in federal and other government grants, expressed "church-state separation" concerns. But their core concern was to prevent any changes in federal law or administrative procedures that might force them either to compete with smaller nonprofits or to start giving the smaller nonprofits that were their own "subrecipients" (and that did most of the actual grant-required work) more than grant-dollar crumbs from their tables.

Writing in 1988, Stuart M. Butler noted that most "government-funded social services in this country are delivered by private contractors, mostly nonprofit organizations."[63] Butler defined "contracting out" as one path to privatization, but he rightly perceived it as a potentially treacherous one:

Not only does contracting use the private sector as an agent of government power and policy, but . . . it creates political and legal dynamics to extend

government further . . . (and) usually leads to pressure from the contractors to increase total government spending on contracts. . . . The phenomenon is
well recognized in the case of weapons procurement
under contract. It is also common in the field of
human services.[64]

Butler's point about the federal contract process was somewhat provocative in 1988, but the same basic point is now
a commonplace observation even in public administration
textbooks. For instance, in a volume published in 2011, the
chapter on "Federal Contracting" reads in part:

The feds' privatization procedures are meant to
ensure, if not efficiency, then at least honesty. In this,
they frequently fail. . . . It is, however, difficult to
overstate the private sector's resistance to acquisitions reform. . . . Washington's lobbyists have grown
in number, sophistication, and clout, and . . . will
challenge any changes that threaten their slurping
at the federal trough.[65]

In 2011, the Project On Government Oversight (POGO)
put a spotlight on federal contracting. The POGO report was
based on an analysis of the total compensation paid to federal
employees versus private sector employees, and on "annual
billing rates for contractor employees across 35 occupational

classifications covering over 550 service activities."[66] POGO cited estimates suggesting that the federal contractor workforce is more than three times the size of the federal employee workforce.[67] POGO concluded that the federal government pays more to hire contractors than it would to hire federal employees to perform the same jobs. Specifically, POGO estimated that federal contractors were paid roughly twice as much as either private workers or federal employees would be paid "for comparable services." While POGO's analysis is not the final word on the subject, and while there are no hard and current data on the number of nonfederal employees whose annual earnings come in whole or in part from federal funds (and even less hard data on the number of nongovernment employees who derive any portion of their earnings from any state, local, or intergovernmental source(s) of funding),[68] there is still no doubting POGO's main observation:

> The federal government has failed to determine how much money it saves or wastes by outsourcing, insourcing, or retaining services, and has no system for doing so.[69]

The U.S. Office of Personnel Management (OPM) is responsible for personnel management of the federal civil service. The OPM's mission statement includes creating and sustaining a world-class workforce for the American people. But the DOD, HHS, VA, EPA, and other contractors that work with the federal workforce are officially beyond the OPM's purview. The first frequently asked question listed on the OPM's "workforce" website concerns whether "OPM data include contractors." OPM's flat-out answer is "no."

Indeed, in testimony before a U.S. Senate Subcommittee on March 29, 2012, Charles D. Grimes III, who was then the OPM's chief operating officer, spoke about "contracting and the multisector workforce."[70] The OPM, he stressed, "does not get involved in agency-specific decisions such as whether or not to competitively source or contract particular functions," and also does not determine whether federal workers "or private contractors are more cost-effective in the performance of government operations."[71] His statement was headed, "Contractors: How Much Are They Costing the Government?" The OPM chief's answer was that his agency could not say, and that "OPM has not delivered training on how agencies should appropriately compare the costs of a contracted versus employed workforce."[72]

In 2013, the U.S. Senate Health, Education, Labor, and Pensions Committee issued a report that documented rampant labor law violations (and worse) by federal contractors and claimed that "many of the functions that private contractors carry out for the government could be done equally well or better by government employees."[73]

For the most part, that view is supported by a small but significant body of recent scholarly research that carefully compares contracted-out or highly outsourced programs to more direct administration or "all bureaucrats" programs.[74] As Melvin J. Dubnick and H. George Frederickson observed in a 2011 report by the National Academy of Public Administration and the Kettering Foundation, when "direct administration programs operated by civil servants" have been compared to comparable grantee- and contractor-laden programs, "in general terms direct government received significantly higher overall" scores for management, effectiveness, and the like.[75] And, beyond proxy government's "important errors, breakdowns, or scandals," the "large-scale outsourcing of the provision of governmental goods and services generally reduces the accountability of government agencies."[76]

CHAPTER 4

If We Knew Then What We Know Now

≳≲

OVER THE LAST half-century, Washington has morphed into the national headquarters for a grotesque form of big government: Leviathan by Proxy. It does not have enough well-trained, public-spirited federal civil servants to do, or to see to it that others do, what federal laws prescribe. For the nobility of public administration it substitutes the imbecility of noncompetitive contracting and "acquisition workforces." It puts Congress where both constitutional propriety and administrative sanity suggest the chief executive should be, and it does so with nary a peep from the federal judiciary. It cannot so much as keep track of what it does and spends. As presently constituted, it cannot dependably or cost-effectively perform core governmental functions or fix long-standing, well-documented administrative problems (including outright fraud) no matter how costly or adverse to public health, wealth, and safety such problems prove to be. Far from doing nothing or doing too little, it does do too much, borrows too much, spends too much, and seduces too many citizens—including too many state and local government officials—into behaving as either its passive dependents or its active supplicants.

Estimable contemporary conservative intellectuals have pondered how to rein in America's big government as they understand it. For example, Charles Murray has proposed replacing the "welfare state" (not just tiny Temporary Assistance to Needy Families but Social Security, Medicare, Medicaid, and all the rest) with an annual $10,000 cash grant to each citizen, starting at age twenty-one, and mandating that each individual spend $3,000 a year on health insurance.[1] In Murray's plan, individuals who make $25,000 per year pay surtaxes on the grant, with those making $50,000 a year or more netting only $5,000 from Uncle Sam. In response to Murray's proposal, some liberals replied, in effect, "make the yearly cash grant closer to $80,000 a year and you've got a deal." But, of course, whatever the annual direct grant number, and whatever the individual mandates or other rules governing health insurance, there will be no such deal, now or ever.

Arthur C. Brooks has lamented "the rise of statism" and Americans' "slide away from the self-governing ideals that Tocqueville found so striking."[2] "The voluntary sector," Brooks has argued, "diminishes as the public sector grows and takes over more functions in people's lives."[3] Brooks is right, but the news is better in some respects (America is still home to more than 60 million citizen-volunteers a year, including a still-robust population of religiously motivated volunteers), and worse, or at least more complicated, in other respects (the "voluntary sector" has been increasingly subsumed by the government-subsidized nonprofit sector, and the nonprofit sector has grown as and because the public sector has grown).

Michael S. Greve has recalled how, after several decades of federal government growth, "the first Reagan administration pursued a broadly Madisonian program."[4] Greve is right that Reagan tried to pump the brakes on big government; but, in constant dollars, the federal government spent 23 percent more in 1989 than it did in 1981. Reagan sought to do three things: (1) increase defense spending, (2) cut taxes, and (3) cut social program spending; he sacrificed the third goal in order to achieve the first two. Reagan's 1986 tax reform deal with Democratic House Speaker Thomas P. "Tip" O'Neill has been hailed as an example of the sort of political compromise that today's Washington policymakers are too polarized to pull off. Actually, it was a "tax less *and* spend more" bargain.

Reagan himself favored a limited but active federal government. For example, there was his famous "There you go again!" quip during an October 25, 1980, debate with President Jimmy Carter, but we forget that he uttered it in reply to Carter's saying that Reagan opposed Medicare and implying that Reagan would seek to reduce or eliminate Washington's role in financing health care. Reagan replied that he opposed the Medicare bill in 1965 because he favored "another piece of legislation" then before Congress that he thought met "the same problem" in a way that "would be better for the senior citizens and provide better care for them than" the bill "that was finally passed."[5] But he was not, he stressed, "opposing the principle of providing care" through federal policies, programs, and regulations.[6]

Many Tea Party supporters and GOP stalwarts mistakenly invoke Reagan when advocating sweeping changes to the Constitution that they claim would put the present-day big government genie back in its pre-1960 bottle. And even the best conservative thinkers generally do not offer either a realistic understanding of the politics that bore, bred, and continue to bolster Leviathan by Proxy or a practical approach to coping with or curing its many serious administrative maladies. But, then again, neither do most liberals or centrist Democrats.

From a progressive's perch, Paul Verkuil has written a serious philosophical, legal, and historical critique about "outsourcing sovereignty."[7] For the most part, however, rightly respected academics at left-leaning universities like Harvard and center-left think tanks like the Brookings Institution have, in effect, learned to love Leviathan by Proxy and professed various concepts and techniques for manipulating or mastering it in the public interest. For instance, leading lights at Harvard have led the charge with "creating public value,"[8] "collaborative governance,"[9] "governing by network,"[10] and other ideas. And my own mid-1990's Brookings Institution corpus (about "deregulating the public service"[11] and so forth) is in much the same tradition. Without meaning to be too critical (including too self-critical), we must ask whether these ideas and analyses amount to more than naming (or renaming) the phenomenon, whistling past huge budget deficits, unduly ignoring or discounting the conservative case for relimiting government, and, in the end, side-stepping all the biggest proxy-management reform challenges (like defense contracting and health care).

And even if we do squarely face up to America's big government as it really is, how, if at all, might it prove possible to both shrink and improve Leviathan by Proxy?

I wish I knew, but perhaps the answer, if there is one, is *more federal bureaucrats, less big government.* And this corollary: *more direct public administration, better government.* It may well be that the only practical way to tame the uniquely American Leviathan's growth while tweaking its performance is to slowly but surely deleverage it by defunding its nonessential proxies and relying more on full-time federal civil servants to directly administer federal policies, programs, and regulations.

Many problems associated with this big government often result from too few federal bureaucrats chasing too many proxies and handling too many dollars. Maybe hiring more federal bureaucrats while pruning proxies would result not only in less big government overall, but also in a federal government that is less beset by grant-seeking and contract-mongering special interests, more faithful to the original Constitution (more "faithfully executed" by the president and less directed by the Congress, with more state and local government agencies that are less like mere federal proxies), more likely to work better and cost less, and less difficult for responsible democratic citizens to hold accountable.

To begin to illuminate this seemingly paradoxical approach to limiting big government's growth while leavening its administration, try a few exercises in counterfactual history.

Imagine that during President Dwight D. Eisenhower's last year in office the Constitution was amended so as to require the federal government to have a balanced budget each year. Would the Ike amendment, as we will call it, have preempted either the expansion of the military-industrial complex, or the rise of the entitlement-nonprofit complex, or the wider growth in government?

Maybe, but "balanced" would not have prohibited taxing lots more while spending lots more. Nor, for that matter, would an amendment that limited federal spending to a given percentage of gross domestic product (GDP) have made much difference. Federal spending as a percentage of GDP was relatively stable from Kennedy through Clinton, but growth in the economy was accompanied by commensurate or greater growth in federal spending.

Now, however, imagine that the Ike amendment did not deal at all with federal spending as such. Rather, imagine that it required the federal government to use only full-time federal employees to administer the policies, programs, and regulations that it legislates and funds.

At the mere mention of such an Ike amendment, both Ike moderates and Barry Goldwater boosters would almost certainly have clutched their chests. Would not such a constitutional amendment be a one-way ticket to a "statist" national government with ever more public employees and ever larger bureaucracies? Any reasonable libertarian, moderate, or even liberal Democrat in the late 1950s or the early 1960s might well have answered, "afraid so."

But what if a crystal ball had permitted them to gaze into the actual future, a half-century hence, in which, for example, about 20 percent of the more than $3.5 trillion annual federal budget was going to pay for citizens' health care (including prescription drugs for senior citizens, and not excluding erectile dysfunction pills for upper-middle class senior citizens) via two federal megaprograms administered by a federal agency that had fewer full-time employees than Harvard University?

What if the same crystal ball had flashed a real future moment in which Washington had tens of thousands of pages of public laws, and was spending scores of billions of dollars each year, on something called the "Department of Homeland Security," which had been hastily cobbled together from twenty-two previously existing federal agencies, and doing so with about as many private contract employees as federal bureaucrats on its payroll? What if the crystal ball also revealed the failed Department of Homeland Security-Federal Emergency Management Agency response to Hurricane Katrina?

Or, what if the crystal ball foretold the future of efforts to delimit federal power by "devolving" federal programs and pushing more federal money into "few strings attached" block grants to the states? Some block grants would be seen to fulfill their promise, but most would be revealed as ways for Washington to spend money that it does not have, for purposes that it does not specify, with results that it does not bother (or have federal bureaucrats bother) to track or measure. On the whole, block grants have not restrained growth in other federal spending, have not reined in federal government authority or expansion, and have not made federal programs more transparent or democratically accountable (in fact, block grants have made them less so).

Finally, what if the crystal ball foreshadowed this can't-make-it-up tidbit? In 2013, the U.S. Department of Agriculture (*Agriculture*) gave tens of thousands of dollars to West Wildwood, a tiny South Jersey beach resort town (*beach resort*), so that it could purchase a sports utility vehicle for its police chief (*police chief*), and the expenditure by the federal agency was considered perfectly routine.[12]

In short, if mid-twentieth-century conservatives could have seen Leviathan by Proxy coming, then they might have guarded themselves against the false hope that a no-growth federal workforce would mean a no-growth or slow-growth federal government.

And if mid-twentieth-century liberals could have gazed over conservatives' shoulders at that same crystal ball, then they might have been less prone to wage and win policy wars on poverty, on environmental protection, and on other issues without planning for the postwar administrative occupation.

In 1973, Jeffrey Pressman and Aaron Wildavsky wrote a now-classic case study showing how a single, small-budget, straightforward, and relatively noncontroversial Great Society economic development project in Oakland, California, was crushed by its own complex administration. The book, *Implementation*, carried a long subtitle that read in part: "Why It's Amazing That Federal Programs Work at All."[13]

In 1988, Donald F. Kettl published his seminal study, *Government by Proxy: (Mis)Managing Federal Programs*. Under the subheading "Inevitable Failures?" Kettl cited Pressman and Wildavsky's book as "the first major work on implementation," and quipped that "implementation studies had become the province of pathologists: analysts who seek to explain why programs die."[14] What he christened "government by proxy" others had previously termed "third-party government"[15] and "indirect administration,"[16] and still others would later relabel (for example, "shadow government,"[17] "hollow state"[18] and "extended state"[19]).

Despite more than two decades' worth of excellent research

that has accompanied all that labeling and relabeling of the government by proxy phenomenon, many basic questions remain unanswered. Indeed, it remains "nearly impossible to come up with more than a guess on" the number of non-federal employees funded in whole or in part by the federal government, "or, for that matter, the number of real federal employees."[20] And, as I intimated previously, even less of a precise character is known about the basic contours of the proxy phenomenon as it exists at the subnational level, including the ratio of subnational government employees to subnational government-funded contractors and grantees.

Still, Kettl's concepts, analyses, and insights have never been surpassed. A quarter-century ago, he was unblinking about how federal contractors were pushing their own agendas. He perceived that, as the federal government spent more and added more issues to its agenda, Washington would increasingly "layer proxies upon proxies."[21] Democratic accountability problems would mount, program failures would multiply, and an already "great political and administrative challenge" would become still greater.[22] The "problems of decentralized, third-party programs" could not, he cautioned, be solved by "a blind retreat to strategies of control—regulation and recentralization," for such a "pathological reflex" to proxy government would probably only make "programs less effective and responsive."[23] Still, he trusted "Americans and their sense of citizenship,"[24] and he concluded the treatise on a cautiously optimistic note:

The litany of program abuses depicted in the media, reinforced by the case studies . . . in this book, may make failure seem inevitable. That, however, is not the message. . . . We have seen triumphs to match the failures and have seen that careful management . . . can lead to success. . . . Government by proxy thus emphasizes with great clarity the obligations of citizenship, for . . . government and its performance depend increasingly on all of us.[25]

CHAPTER 5

More Federal Bureaucrats, Less Big/ Bad Government

—— ≥≤ ——

AMERICA HAS BEEN aptly described as "the first new nation."[1] America continues to be an exceptional nation,[2] and America's representative democracy is now home to an exceptionally diverse people.

But the health of any great republic depends ultimately on its citizens' civic character—their discernment in deciding who governs in addition to their self-discipline, prudence, and compassion in deciding what should be done by individuals and families, what should be done by churches and other civil society institutions, what should be done by businesses through free or mostly free markets, and what should be done by which policymakers and public servants at which levels of government. As goes any free people's civic character, so, in the end, goes their freedom, their prosperity, and their posterity.

Mistrust and bellow about the federal government though they do, most Americans believe what President Franklin

Delano Roosevelt believed about the federal government: namely, that it can and should not only defend us against foreign enemies, but also actively seek to create the conditions under which average Americans can lead peaceful and productive, if not uniformly prosperous, lives. Persistent public majorities have strongly favored having not only national defense, but also income security, health care, environmental protection, housing, education, and more on Washington's agenda.

As E. J. Dionne Jr. has observed, Americans "believe in limited government, but also in active government. Our Founders did not devote so much time and energy to creating a strong federal government only for it to do nothing."[3]

Amen. But rather than being the strong yet limited government the Founders would have wanted for twenty-first-century Americans, today's federal government is at once hyperactive and anemic, overgrown and understaffed—not at all what this great republic's federal government could and should be.

Still, let me end not with a counsel of despair, but on a note of cautious optimism (or at least not outright pessimism). It is easier to sing the blues than it is to offer a blueprint for a more limited and better big government. But, for whatever it might be worth, and without self-censoring in strict accordance with political feasibility considerations, here is a highly preliminary "to-do" list for shrinking and improving Leviathan by Proxy.

Revive the Administrative Presidency

The place to begin is 1600 Pennsylvania Avenue.

Writing a half-year before problems with "health exchange" websites and such became headline news, *Time* magazine's Joe Klein saw the problems coming and warned that "Obamacare will fail" unless the White House started paying "more attention to the details of implementation."[4] For his trouble, Klein, who in other columns had criticized the Obama administration for not getting a handle on major administrative problems at the Department of Veterans Affairs, got an audience with the president and an earful from several West Wing presidential advisers. The new health care law's implementation problems, they insisted, would not be nearly so bad as his warning foretold.[5] They were right—the problems proved to be even worse than Klein had anticipated.

By May 2014, just about everyone, including President Obama and his team, had admitted as much, but it remained unclear just how much new and improved attention to implementation matters the White House was mustering, not only on Obamacare but on myriad other major administrative challenges including huge problems at VA-run hospitals. In an essay entitled "The Reluctant Executive," Donald F. Kettl warned that the administration was falling fast into the "Katrina syndrome—stumbling into big management problems and then failing to solve them."[6] He also stated the consequences of this syndrome: "Failing to pay attention to public administration could cripple not only" the president's "health reform legacy," but also "spill over into large swaths of the executive branch."[7]

But, as the name "Katrina syndrome" might indicate, and as Kettl stressed, Obama would hardly be the first president of the modern era to have his presidency marred or worse by failing to fix major management and implementation problems. The "gap between political and governing realities," he noted, "is nothing new."[8] He recommended several things the administration could do before 2016 to prevent the worst from happening, including "Put someone in charge and back them up."[9]

As usual, Kettl was right; but, if the decades-old dilemmas wrought by Leviathan by Proxy are going to be addressed in ways that really make a long and lasting difference, then the "someone in charge" now and in the decades ahead, the person at the highest level who pays attention to public administration, must be none other, and none below, the president of the United States.

The Constitution established a federal government with three coequal branches and created what Richard E. Neustadt described as a "system of separated institutions sharing powers."[10] Article I of the Constitution makes Congress "the first branch" of the federal government, outlining congressional powers. It is about twice as long as Article II (the executive branch) and Article III (the federal judiciary) combined. But, when it comes to executing federal laws, the Constitution distinctly makes Congress a distant second to the president. Article II begins: "The executive Power shall be vested in a President of the United States of America."

Political scientists generally date the rise of the "modern presidency" either to the administration of Theodore "Teddy" Roosevelt or to that of Franklin Delano Roosevelt. But, albeit to varying degrees, presidents from George Washington to Dwight D. Eisenhower functioned in no small measure as chief executive. In what most scholars rank as an otherwise undistinguished presidency, Chester A. Arthur, who served from 1881 to 1885, is nonetheless widely credited with pushing against the patronage system and putting the federal government on a path to what became the federal civil service "merit" system.[11]

Even into the mid-twentieth century, presidents and their senior staffs spent significant time on matters pertaining to the administration of federal laws. But the last president who functioned more than incidentally as a chief administrator was Eisenhower (a habit that he could not shake, having planned, organized, staffed, and budgeted the military to accomplish little chores like D-day). For the last half-century, presidents have instead functioned ever more as chief legislators, chief agenda-setters, or chief communicators, and ever less as chief administrators (Richard Nixon's efforts to gain political control of the bureaucracy do not count).

Today, the West Wing and the Executive Office of the President is organized in ways that reflect the demise of the administrative presidency and the rise of what Jeffrey K. Tulis has described as the "rhetorical presidency."[12] The Press Secretary's Office, the Communications Office, the Domestic Policy Council, and other such offices are all in the president's inner-circle.[13] Even in administrative crisis situations, senior staff members reflexively work to keep the president from getting down "in the weeds" of administrative details (think of George W. Bush and FEMA during the early days of Hurricane Katrina or Barack Obama during the months before the launch of "health exchanges"). Instead, presidents wage a "permanent campaign," and the White House senior staff (assistants to the president), other commissioned officers (deputy and special assistants to the president), and the rest of the 3,000-plus presidential political appointees function for the most part as *political* appointees, not professional public administrators.

Reviving the administrative presidency is a necessary but insufficient condition for significantly limiting, repairing, and improving Leviathan by Proxy. The "permanent campaign" itself can be drafted into the cause if the people and the press hold all the president's men and women responsible for what "the federal bureaucracy" does even when we are not watching a major city go under water or experiencing "computer glitches" by the millions.

While I share Theodore J. Lowi's nostalgia for the aforementioned *Schechter* rule (forbidding the delegation and redelegation of legislative powers to administrative officials), it has now been more than seven decades since the rule was taken at all seriously by Article III's federal judiciary. Still, if conservative legal beagles want a worthwhile challenge (one that would benefit the public in the long run more than the nth federal lawsuit over Obamacare), they should mount challenges in the federal courts against especially egregious examples of delegated legislative powers and especially rank exercises of bureaucratic and proxy-administration discretion.

And, while there is nobody that loves James Madison more than I do, the Founder that we need to rally to now is not Madison but Alexander Hamilton. Madisonian constitution-alism was glorious while it lasted, and it lasted for about 170 years—warts, civil war, and all. But since the 1960s, the Madisonian system has broken down. There is, however, an alternative constitutional framework for sustaining a limited but active big government. The alternative is right there in *The Federalist Papers* alongside Madison's best ideas about constitutional theory and practice: Hamiltonian republi-canism. In the presidency-focused *Federalist Paper* No. 70, Hamilton writes:

> Energy in the executive is a leading character in the
> definition of good government. It is essential to the
> protection of the community against foreign attacks;
> it is not less essential to the steady administration of
> the laws; to the protection of property against those

irregular and high-handed combinations which
sometimes interrupt the ordinary course of justice;
to the security of liberty against the enterprises and
assaults of ambition, of faction, and of anarchy.[14]

HIRE 1 MILLION MORE FULL-TIME CIVIL SERVANTS BY 2035

The ambition, faction, and administrative anarchy of Leviathan by Proxy is manifest (1) in routine administrative dysfunctions, failures, and not-infrequent fiascoes; (2) in how
the federal contracting process has malfunctioned or been
corrupted; and (3) in how so many proxies function as lobbies for laws that line their own pockets without also serving
the public interest. There can be no full or partial cure for this
disease without such "energy in the executive" as might come
from having a full-time federal workforce with enough well-
trained, well-motivated civil servants to faithfully execute the
laws as directed by the chief executive.

In 1965, the ratio of full-time federal civil servants (around
1.9 million), excluding uniformed military personnel and
postal workers, to the total U.S. population (about 193 million) was about 1 federal bureaucrat for every 100 citizens.
In 2013, with a civilian workforce around 2.1 million and a
total U.S. population around 316 million that same ratio was
about 1 federal bureaucrat for every 150 citizens.

The U.S. Census Bureau estimates that the nation's population in 2035 will be about 370 million.[15] If the federal workforce grew back up to its 1965 ratio, then by 2035 it would have about 3.6 million employees. If, instead, the federal workforce merely maintained its 2013 ratio, then by 2035 it would have about 2.5 million workers. The midpoint between the two growth trajectories would land the federal personnel roster at about 3 million by 2035, with roughly 1 federal bureaucrat for every 125 citizens.

Crude as it is, that calculation is probably in the ballpark of what's needed: 1 million more full-time federal civilian workers by 2035.

Based on the Clinton-Gore 1993–2001 record and on the Obama-Biden 2009–14 record, there is no reason to think that future Democratic presidential administrations would be more prone to push for a steady and significant expansion in the federal workforce than future Republican presidential administrations would be. The federal workforce shrunk under Clinton-Gore. In his 2011 State of the Union address, President Obama reiterated his campaign pledge to shrink the federal bureaucracy and joked about its inefficiency: "The Interior Department is in charge of salmon while they're in fresh water, but the Commerce Department handles them when they're in salt water. And I hear it gets even more complicated once they're smoked."

In actuality, during the first five years of the Obama administration, including two years in which the federal workforce fell, the number of federal bureaucrats increased on net by about 50,000.[16] Yet, reinforcing the pattern dating back to the 1960s, the federal budget grew faster than the federal workforce did. As figure 2 shows, in constant dollars, federal spending per federal bureaucrat reached new peaks. As Kettl has observed, "More federal employees were responsible not for managing programs but for managing proxies who managed programs on government's behalf."[17]

FIGURE 2. LEVERAGE INDEX: FEDERAL SPENDING PER FEDERAL BUREAUCRAT

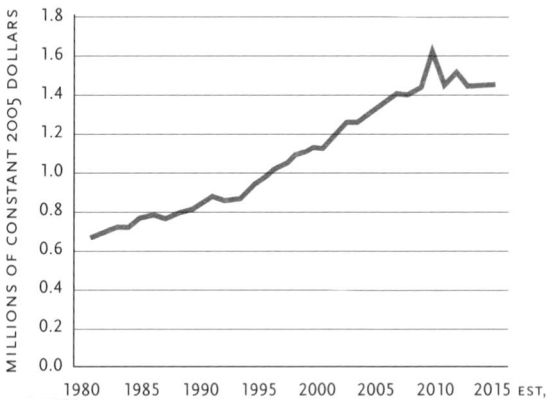

Source: Donald F. Kettl, "From Intergovernmental to Intersectoral" (unpublished paper, 2014), 14, calculated in constant 2005 dollars from U.S. Office of Management and Budget, Budget of the U.S. Government: Fiscal Year 2014—Historical Tables.

As we have seen with respect to federal programs and agencies as diverse as the Federal Emergency Management Agency, the Environmental Protection Agency, the Social

Security Administration, and others, each federal bureaucrat has not only been handling far more money but also doing more tasks and managing more proxies. Were the 1980–2015 line in figure 2 somehow weighted to reflect not just the increase in federal dollars but also the increase in the size, scope, and complexity of federal "public administration" in the age of Leviathan by Proxy—more dollars, more beneficiaries, more proxies, more programs, more tasks—Kettl's federal public administration's "leverage index" would be even steeper.

Under the budget proposed by President Obama in 2014, federal employment would increase by 14,000 in 2015.[18] But to increase the full-time federal civilian workforce by 1 million employees over the next two decades—an average of 50,000 a year for each of the next 20 years—would mean increasing it in each of those years as much as it increased on net from January 2009 through March 2014.

As table 2 makes plain, the number of federal bureaucrats varies among and between cabinet departments and independent agencies. But regardless of their respective workforce totals, some federal departments and agencies need a bigger workforce just to begin to catch up to a workload that has grown bigger over the decades and others need more or accelerated hires to cope with new duties or larger citizen-client populations that are already mounting or definitely coming. And almost all need more people to more effectively monitor, manage, and measure the performance of their proxies. The

TABLE 2. NUMBER OF FEDERAL CIVILIAN EMPLOYEES,* 2010

Defense	772,000
Veterans Affairs	313,000
Homeland Security	191,000
Justice	118,000
Treasury	113,000
Agriculture	98,000
Health and Human Services	84,000
Interior	72,000
Social Security Administration	70,000
Independent Agencies**	68,000**
Transportation	58,000
Commerce	45,000
Environmental Protection Agency	19,000
NASA	19,000
Energy	17,000
Labor	17,000
General Services Administration	13,000
State	12,000
Housing and Urban Development	10,000
Education	5,000
TOTAL	2.1 Million

*Rounded to nearest 1,000

**All excluding SSA, EPA, NASA, and GSA, each of which is listed here separately

Source: Adapted from Curtis W. Copeland, *The Federal Workforce: Characteristics and Trends* (Washington, DC: Congressional Research Service, April 19, 2011), 6, table 4, reporting data from OPM's FedScope database.

expansion in federal hiring, were it to happen at all, would be most efficacious if it was front-loaded so that more than half of the increase occurred over the next decade, starting with the Social Security Administration and other federal bureaucracies with unambiguous needs for more workers now. And help-wanted signs should be hung out now for the assorted units within federal agencies that specialize in contract planning, awarding, and overseeing.

Where they come into play, government employee unions should be prevailed upon to make major, long-term, flexibility-enhancing, efficiency-promoting concessions in order to make the workforce expansion happen.

Drain the For-Profit Federal Contracting Swamps

But hiring more federal bureaucrats will not limit and improve Leviathan by Proxy unless it is coupled with efforts to limit and clean up the federal contracting process. If your business, whether it is a small company or a multinational megacorporation, gets government money to do the people's business, then, during the entire period that the work is being performed, your business should not be allowed to lobby Congress in any way that relates to renewing its federal contracts, enriching its federal contracts, or being awarded additional federal contracts—period.

Federal contracts to profit-making firms should be subject

to award caps. Whether the caps are calibrated as a percentage of the company's gross annual revenues (e.g., the award cannot constitute more than 50 percent of total company earnings), as a percentage of the total funding for the relevant line item of the agency's budget, or in other ways, the objective is to keep companies from depending excessively on federal funding to meet their payrolls and furnish their suites. Especially in defense contracting, many companies are de facto federal agencies. Uncapped contracting brought this military-industrial complex into being—end it.

By the same token, the epidemic of one-bid "competition" needs to end. If there is a compelling public interest in giving a single business a multimillion-dollar or multibillion-dollar, multiyear federal contract, then let us not leave that important decision to undertrained, understaffed acquisition workforce bureaucrats.

Require a literal and separate act of Congress for each and every sole source deal above a certain dollar value (try $25 million, for starters), and let the public see what "the contracting process" hides. The fresh sunlight might prove to be a disinfectant for corruption, a tonic that prevents planned cost overruns, and so on.

Taking vendor past performance into account is a must, but that cannot happen in the full sense until vendors that previously violated federal laws are not merely wrist-slapped with trivial fines but duly disciplined and displaced from the contracting process for real.

In a March 4, 2009, "Memorandum for the Heads of Executive Departments and Agencies," President Obama insisted that the federal government "must have sufficient capacity to manage and oversee the contracting process from start to finish."

Amen. But, as noted in chapter three, the Office of Personnel Management (OPM) does not keep data on contractors. A new, specialized federal office should be created to gather and disseminate systematic data on contractor personnel, productivity, and compliance.

GIVE GRANTS FOR NONPROFIT
ORGANIZATIONS' NONMEMBERS ONLY

Tax-exempt organizations constitute what is sometimes called the "independent sector," but many among the nation's more than 1.6 million nonprofit organizations are highly dependent on government in at least four ways: (1) they own tax-exempt property, (2) they receive tax-deductible donations, (3) they receive government grants and contracts, and (4) they have beneficiaries or clients who receive government support and fork it over to the nonprofit body.

For instance, a typical well-endowed private university own tens of millions of dollars in property that goes untaxed; collects tens of millions of dollars a year in contributions donated by alumni who deduct the donations on their federal income tax returns; receives six- and seven-figure government grants and contracts as a recipient, subrecipient, or vendor (for example, the American Recovery and Reinvestment Act of 2009 was especially generous to many private universities); and enrolls students who pay tuition with government-supplied grants or loans.

Most private universities, however, do more than just hold on-campus arts and sciences classes. Many now have robust community-serving programs and benefit people who are not their own students, faculty, staff, or alumni. By the same token, many giant nonprofit organizations, both religious and secular, are civic treasures, and there are tiny, community-serving, street-level nonprofit organizations (like many urban congregations) that work "loaves and fishes" miracles with whatever funding, public or private, they receive. And many private grant-making foundations give away good money to achieve good purposes in education, health, and other public-spirited spheres.

Still, what the public actually gets in return for all the rest of the nonprofit sector's public supports and subsidies, and how tax-exempt organizations are held accountable, are matters that have begun to attract more serious attention from both policymakers and scholars alike. And, alas, billions of dollars in government support also goes to nonprofit organizations that use tax dollars to pay their own staff's salaries and benefits without clearly benefitting people other than those in their own workforces or to subsidize activities, programs, or facilities that are not plainly related to the nonprofits' core missions or main justifications for tax-exempt status.

Whether via a revitalized Internal Revenue Service (IRS) or via a new federal agency created for the purpose, federal grants to tax-exempt organizations, starting with grants that are explicitly for "human services," need to be scrutinized more routinely and more systematically in relation to how, if at all, they measurably benefit nonmembers.

What the Independent Sector, in announcing a July 2014 training program,[19] referred to as "nonprofit advocacy and lobbying" has become so pervasive, and the pressure on so many government grant-dependent nonprofit leaders to forge "strong relationships with public officials and their staffs" has become so acute, that either the IRS or a new federal agency needs to help the nation's overwhelmingly well-intentioned nonprofit board members and executives to ensure that their respective tax-exempt organizations are not inadvertently politicking in ways that they should not.

At the same time, however, both elected and appointed public officials at all levels of government need to hear what both the Independent Sector and the National Council of Nonprofits has counseled over the years regarding government's often perverse and wasteful nonprofit grant-monitoring processes and protocols. For instance, they should heed what the Council recommended in a May 15, 2014 report regarding the need to "reduce redundant monitoring" by "multiple government agencies" while "standardizing and integrating reporting procedures."[20]

More generally, *all* organizations that receive federal grants or contracts—nonprofit organizations, for-profit firms, and state and local government agencies—should be required to report in exacting but straightforward detail on how many full-time or part-time employees, including any subcontractor or subrecipient organizations' employees, receive salaries and benefits that are paid in whole or in part with federal monies.

Take Federalism Back to the Future: Freeze, and Then Reinvent, Grants-in-Aid

In 1960, federal grants to state and local governments were designed to serve essentially state and local purposes. In 2011, Washington spent about $625 billion on grants to the state and local governments.[21] As noted earlier, adjusted for inflation, that was more than ten times the amount that the federal government granted them in 1960.[22] As figure 3 indicates, the big post-1960 growth in federal grants to state and local governments was accompanied by big changes in the grants' purposes. In 1960, the two biggest federal grants-in-aid items were transportation and highways grants (43 percent) and income security grants (38 percent). By 2011, Medicaid, which did not exist until 1965, was by far the largest grant category (46 percent) followed by income security (19 percent), education and training (15 percent), and transportation and highways (10 percent).

The dramatic increase in federal grants to state and local governments, and the dramatic shifts in what federal grant-in-aid dollars fund, began when federal politicians, not state and local ones, began devising "revenue sharing" programs based less on what state and local officials were demanding and

FIGURE 3. FEDERAL GRANTS TO STATE
AND LOCAL GOVERNMENTS, 1960 AND 2011

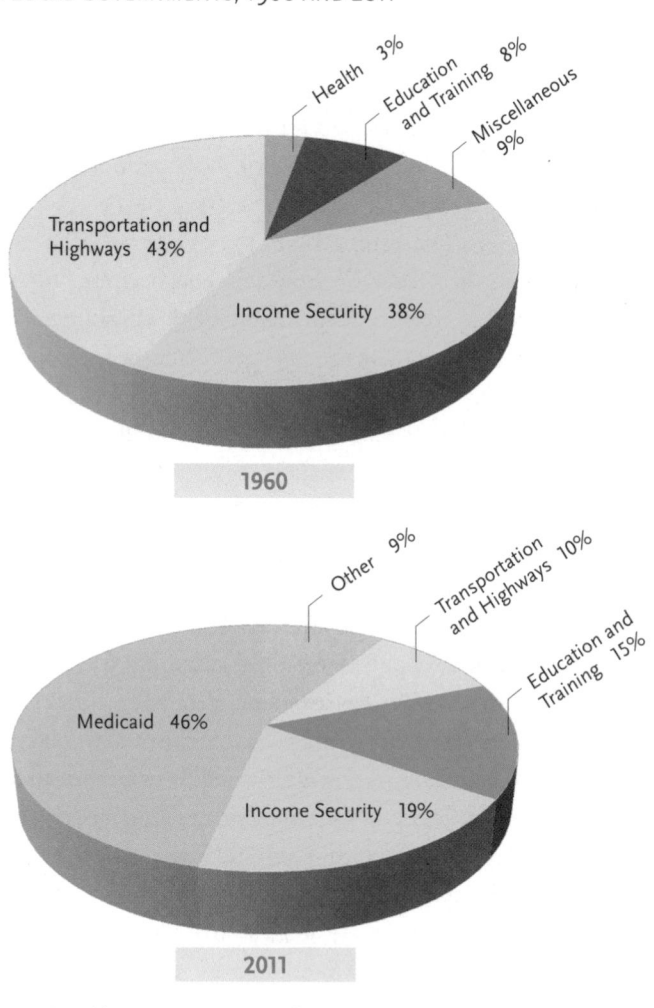

Health 3%

Education
and Training 8%

Miscellaneous
9%

Transportation and
Highways 43%

Income Security 38%

1960

Other 9%

Transportation
and Highways 10%

Education and
Training 15%

Medicaid 46%

Income Security 19%

2011

Source: Data derived from Congressional Budget Office, *Federal Grants to State and Local Governments* (Washington, DC, March 2013), 2–4.

more on what federal policymakers deemed to be national needs. Federal leaders were the principal proponents of grant-in-aid programs to reduce poverty, combat crime, improve education, and more. In response, state and local officials took the money, but also asked for, and got, more money for their own priorities.

By the 1980s, after about two decades of ceaseless expansion, the "federal" programs had become "intergovernmental" in all ways that mattered, both politically and administratively. But, at the same moment, the federal money began to dry up or slow down. Washington began foisting ever more "unfunded mandates" on the states even as it also pushed more block grants their way. Over the last quarter-century, the U.S. Conference of Mayors, the National Governors Association, and other state and local government groups have functioned as part of an intergovernmental lobby. The purpose of the intergovernmental lobby has been the same as that of any private lobby: to obtain more federal money with fewer strings attached.

Most federal grants to states go, in the end, to individual citizens as payments for unemployment benefits, health insurance supplied via Medicaid, supplemental nutrition programs including so-called food stamps, and more. Growth in those federal funds need not be restricted in order to freeze at 2014 levels most other federal grants-in-aid, starting with federal dollars that are used to expand state corrections departments, city commercial development corporations, and so on.

Leviathan by Proxy cannot be contained, and cannot be made to work better and cost less, without efforts to return to the days when the administration of federal programs depended less than it does now on state and local government proxies, and when governors, mayors, and subnational government agency heads looked less to Washington and more to the state capital or city hall for both direction and funding.

As Alice Rivlin has observed, because federal housing, public health, education, homeland security, and many other programs program are "administered by the state or locality" with funds that "are comingled with money from other sources, there is no way for citizens to know which level of government to hold accountable for results."[23]

The next president should sponsor a bipartisan presidential commission to reinvent federal grants-in-aid by "swapping" certain functions among and between different levels of government, like, to cite one possible proposal, the feds taking all the Medicaid action in return for the states doing without federal funding for education.

WAKE-UP CALL FOR WE THE PEOPLE

In sum, over the last half-century, the federal government increased its spending more than fivefold while the full-time federal civilian workforce remained largely flat. Washington was not only spending lots more, but also doing lots more on everything while tackling issues and problems that had previously not been on the federal agenda. Still, the number of federal bureaucrats did not increase accordingly. In fact, during some post-1960 periods, while the federal government expanded (more spending, more borrowing, and more policies, programs, and regulations on more issues), the federal workforce actually shrank. State and local government employees, for-profit contractors, and nonprofit grantees frequently administered federal laws. The state and local government workforce more than tripled. Nonprofit organizations proliferated and added people to their payrolls as government grant dollars poured in. The big government that resulted is today debt financed, proxy administered, deeply dysfunctional, and an anathema to the nation's finest constitutional and democratic traditions.

Maybe, however, with a slowly but surely revived administrative presidency, a million more full-time civil servants by 2035, a reformed and downsized federal contracting process, new protocols that steer federal grants away from nonprofit organizations that do not plainly benefit nonmembers, and an effort to reinvent the federal grants-in-aid system, America's big government might become less big, less bad, and more likely to be a blessing than a burden to ourselves and our posterity.

But make no mistake: Leviathan by Proxy is here to stay. Nobody truly knows how to predictably and reliably slow its growth or improve its performance. It is past time for We the People to understand it—and to accept responsibility for it.

PART 2

❈

Dissenting Points of View

CHAPTER 6

The Government We Need for the Things We Want

— ⊱⊰ —

E. J. Dionne Jr.

A CANDIDATE FOR the highest office in the land whose central campaign theme was a pledge to restore the "administrative presidency" would be met with dismissive chuckles by every pundit and political consultant in the nation. If another candidate said that the only way to reduce the size of government was to hire 1 million additional federal bureaucrats, cable television hosts would scour the nation for psychiatrists and other practitioners of the therapeutic arts to call that politician's sanity into question.

Adventurous thinkers exist to confound us and, in the process, require us to examine familiar problems in ways that our conventional assumptions won't let us consider. John DiIulio's freestyle mix of ideas from left and right performs this service brilliantly. He focuses on questions that most elected officials (for the reasons outlined above) are reluctant, even petrified, to talk much about. Here is hoping that his lively provocation moves three important ideas into the mainstream discussion.

First, we need a wholesale reexamination of our habit of outsourcing the federal government's functions—the "government by proxy" system that is at the heart of DiIulio's critique. There is certainly a case for grants to state and local governments and also a need for contracting certain services that the government lacks the expertise to perform or doesn't need to perform regularly. But as DiIulio shows with a blizzard of facts and figures, we have allowed the system to get out of hand. Does it really make sense, for example, that the Department of Defense has the equivalent of 710,000 full-time contract employees alongside 800,000 civilian workers? We need a resolutely practical and nonideological review of whether we are delegating and contracting out functions of the federal government that could be performed more efficiently and more responsively by people who actually work for it and are directly accountable to it.

Second, we cannot have either responsive or efficient government if we pretend that the enterprise can function well without an adequate number of employees. We have chosen to have a large government but have not provided ourselves the means of running it. Instead, DiIulio writes, there are "too few federal bureaucrats chasing too many proxies and handling too many dollars" (p. 83). He also calls our attention to the large number of experienced civil servants who will be retiring over the next decade. Where is the inspired and inspiring effort to recruit the new (and young) talent federal agencies must hire in the coming decades? Without such an effort, the government's performance will slowly and quietly deteriorate.

Third, we need the president of the United States to take far more seriously the task of reforming and then running the operations of government. It's hard to imagine anyone ever winning an election on the slogan: "Better Administration, for the People." But until administration looms larger as a White House priority, no president will succeed in breaking the cycle of mistrust and cynicism that is poisoning our politics and distancing so many of our citizens from public life.

In arguing for a larger number of federal employees, DiIulio says that one of his purposes is to reduce the size of government. His case for this counterintuitive claim rests on the sensible idea that proxy government will continue to spiral out of control in the absence of proper supervision. But cutting back government is not my cause because I do not believe that the percentage of the gross domestic product (GDP) consumed by government is a good measure of our freedom—or lack thereof. For this ever to be the case, government's take from the private sector would have to reach a point that is currently unimaginable in our capitalist democracy. That's true even though government will inevitably consume a somewhat higher proportion of national income over the next three decades as baby boomers retire.

Because I don't believe that the current or likely size of the

American state is a threat to our liberty, my principal dissent from DiIulio's argument is his use of the term "Leviathan" to describe the current government of our constitutional republic. The word is biblical in origin, associated with sea monsters. The book of Isaiah refers to Leviathan as a "coiling serpent." Thanks to the philosopher Thomas Hobbes, the word has come to refer to an autocratic state.

DiIulio correctly notes that in 2013, the federal government spent five times more than it spent in 1960, adjusting the numbers for inflation. But the main drivers of this growth are the nation's health care programs (there was no Medicare or Medicaid in 1960), steady cost of living increases in Social Security, and a much older population. Military expenditure has also grown in absolute terms, though it represents a lower share of GDP. Are these threats to our freedom?

By way of dramatizing government's reach, DiIulio invites us to "just try to name ten adult U.S. citizens you know who have never received any federal, state, local, or intergovernmental government payments, loans, subsidies, grants, contracts or other benefits whatsoever" (p. 42).

Well, sure. All of us will have trouble finding those ten. To which I reply, as politely as possible: So what? All the adults we know who are over sixty-five are on Social Security and Medicare. Every homeowner benefits from the tax subsidy of mortgage interest payments. A vast number of college students have received subsidized loans and scholarships. Widows and their children receive survivor's benefits. (I was

among them after my father died.) Every soldier, police officer, firefighter, teacher, social worker, park ranger—in other
words, every village, town, city, county, state, and federal
worker in the country—is paid by some level of government.

One can debate this or that policy, the size and efficacy
of various programs, the utility and fairness of our many
subsidies. But as a general matter, I see no reason why our
nation should be troubled by the fact that it provides for
the elderly and (usually inadequately) for the poor or that
it invests in important public goods. The test of whether we
have a Leviathan state is not how big it is, but what it does.
Through most of our history, Americans have used government to empower rather than to oppress.

But DiIulio's use of the term has an important virtue: it
dramatizes his point that "Americans do indeed hate 'big
government,'" but also "love, love, *love* federal government goods, services, and benefits" (p. 29). For this reason,
he argues, politicians have disguised the ways they have
increased the size of governments to meet the voters' wants.
Rather than hiring people at the federal level, they make
sure the bodies are counted elsewhere. DiIulio cites Martha
Derthick's compact explanation of this strategy (p. 35). Congress, she says, "has resolved this dilemma by turning over
the bulk of administration to the state governments or any
organizational instrumentality it can lay its hands on whose
employees are not counted on the federal payroll" (p. 35).

Again, there is nothing irrational about providing federal

support to state and local governments or to charitable groups. (I suspect I am less troubled by some of these programs than is DiIulio who, as long-time supporter of the good work of faith-based organizations, has his own ambivalences.) And government will always have to buy goods from the outside. We don't need government-run cement factories to build our highways or federal buildings.

But DiIulio is entirely convincing in showing us that an obsession with the raw number of bureaucrats on the payroll is plainly stupid. It leads politicians to brag about cutting even necessary jobs from the federal workforce, something they do even as they encourage proxies to do even more hiring through the backdoor. Then they brag about how many jobs they have created.

Good for DiIulio for recognizing that "bureaucrats" are actually public servants who perform work necessary for a more responsive and, yes, more efficient government. Cutting the Internal Revenue Service workforce when some $450 billion in taxes owed go uncollected is precisely the opposite of what a journeyman economist or efficiency expert would suggest. By boosting collections, additional Internal Revenue Service agents would *cut* the deficit—and make the system more just for those who obey the law and pay what they owe. And does it take genius to wonder how well the Social Security Administration will perform if its workforce is cut at a time when the number of Americans receiving benefits will rise from 62 million to 85 million?

For all of DiIulio's warnings about Leviathan, he plainly has a passion for a government that works and for programs that succeed. He cites his teacher Don Kettl's insistence that while government failure gets most of the attention from the media (and, in truth, from academic students of bureaucracies), "[w]e have seen triumphs to match the failures" and that "careful management . . . can lead to success" (p. 89). Wouldn't it be nice to have a political version of Lent during which members of Congress would give up arguments about "big" and "small" government and devote at least forty days to discussing instead efficient government, effective government, and responsive government? DiIulio has provided them with a text to guide their reflections.

One would also like to think that President Barack Obama might read this book before he leaves office and give the administrative side of his job attention he did not afford it earlier. (The experience of the HealthCare.gov website does seem to have concentrated his attention on such matters.) Those who want to succeed him might find the administrative presidency more exciting than they imagined. And voters, in whose name these elected officials act, could ponder anew whether they are willing to support the government they need to get the things that they want.

CHAPTER 7

No Cure for the Sclerotic State

≥≤

Charles Murray

JOHN DIIULIO has handed up the first half of the indict-
ment. The federal Leviathan by Proxy is every bit as dysfunctional as he portrayed it. Now let me enter the other half:
the federal government administered by full-time bureaucrats is just as dysfunctional. The problems that DiIulio has
identified are not the result of a federal workforce too small
for the important tasks it has been assigned, but a federal
government that has reached an advanced stage of sclerosis.

In his seminal book, *The Logic of Collective Action*, the
late economist Mancur Olson explained that an inescapable
problem in all democratic societies is the power of small
interest groups to get their way at the expense of the public good.[1] Why has the sugar subsidy persisted decade after
decade, raising the price of sugar for all Americans while
benefitting a comparatively tiny number of sugar producers?
Because of an asymmetry of incentives: the sugar producers

are powerfully motivated to maintain their large benefit from the subsidy, while the average American is weakly motivated to get a lower price on sugar. Olson generalized these dynamics to all government programs that have important benefits for a limited group of recipients while exacting small and often hidden costs on the population as a whole.

In 1982, Olson built on his theory in *The Rise and Decline of Nations*.[2] Over time, the number and influence of groups formed to advance their own interests through the use of government inevitably grow. Few of these groups have an interest in increasing the size of the economic pie. It's much easier for them to seek benefits by cutting out a larger piece of the existing pie for itself. How? Sometimes directly as a subsidy, as a tax exemption for its members, or as a rule that benefits them and not their competitors. Sometimes indirectly by hobbling the competition. Many large corporations are quietly enthusiastic about the administrative state because they have the political clout to shape legislation and regulatory rulemaking to their advantage and the financial and personnel resources to cope with government requirements that overwhelm smaller competitors. The notorious Dodd-Frank bill to regulate the financial industry, excoriated by many businesspeople and economists as the worst kind of incomprehensible, needlessly burdensome regulation, is a case in point. As the chairman of JP Morgan admitted with remarkable candor, which he has probably come to regret, Dodd-Frank works as a "bigger moat" to protect the large investment banks like JP Morgan, deterring smaller institutions from entering JP Morgan's markets.[3]

Meanwhile, the regulators themselves have a vested interest in opposing simplification or reductions in their "product"—and indeed, a vested interest in legislation that further expands their "customer" base. The U.S. Environmental Protection Agency and the Occupational Safety and Health Administration do not celebrate when companies assimilate the old regulations so that EPA and OSHA no longer have anything to complain about. Instead, they look for more things to complain about.

Olson argued that every time this pie reslicing goes on, the society as a whole systematically becomes poorer—reslicing not only fails to increase the size of the pie, it exacts costs that shrink it. Eventually such a government becomes sclerotic, as Olson put it—a word that evokes a remarkably apt analogy with a hardening of the arteries and nerves of the body politic. The descriptions of the dysfunctions in John DiIulio's essay read like case studies of Olson's theory in practice.

When Olson articulated his theory of national decline at the beginning of the 1980s, the process was already well underway. It has since progressed much further, as journalist Jonathan Rauch has described in *Government's End*.[4] With regard to Leviathan by Proxy, these points seem most salient:

Within the administrative state, the core functions—the ones that I could agree should be administered by full-time federal employees—have been swamped by others that range from silly to destructive. How can I convey that in a few paragraphs? Many books tell the story in detail.[5] But instead, you could do a little exploration on your own to convince yourself that the administrative state has run amok. Take, for example, the regulation of workplaces. Even a libertarian like me won't go to the wall to prevent regulations that increase the safety of tunnels in coal mines or of work areas near whirring buzz saws. But if you leaf through the pages of the *Code of Federal Regulations* (174,545 of them as of 2012) the regulations that fall in the category of "Thank heavens the government is overseeing this" will be swamped by ones that, for example, prescribe the permissible heights of counters in the deli departments of grocery stores.[6] Or you may Google whatever business comes to mind along with the words "OSHA" or "EPA" and take a look at some sample regulations for yourself. My search haphazardly brought up dentists' offices. I discovered that to find out how to comply with government regulations affecting dentists, an *OSHA Manual for Dentists* is on sale for just $189. It takes 283 pages to describe the applicable regulations.[7] But you'll be glad to know that your $189 also buys you a "Do-It-Yourself Documentation Kit" that will enable you to "prepare your facility for OSHA inspection." It is ninety-seven pages long. I bet you didn't realize how dangerous dentist's offices were before the government got involved.

You might also do some exploration of the unfathomable labyrinth that federal bureaucracies have become. I went to the website for the Department of Energy (DOE) (a juicy target, but any other cabinet department would do) and found its organization chart. As of 2013, three undersecretaries reported to the Office of the Secretary of Energy. Combined, those three undersecretaries ran twenty-nine separate offices, most of them headed by a deputy administrator or associate administrator. In addition, the heads of fifteen other offices report directly to the Office of the Secretary—forty-four in all.

While examining this chart, I accidentally clicked on one of those forty-four entities, the Office of Health Safety and Security, and found that I had formerly reached only the lobby of the bureaucratic maze. The Office of Health Safety and Security had five divisions reporting to the chief. The heads of those divisions had a total of thirty-seven offices reporting to them. And lest you think that "office" by the time you get this deep into the organizational maze means literally a single office with just one person in it, all of them had directors and staffs of unknown size. We're looking at hundreds—I didn't try to count them all—of entities within the DOE alone. And, as you have learned from reading John DiIulio, they probably have contracts with private firms that augmented their staffs by proxy. Throughout the exercise, as I read so many meaningless titles of offices and incomprehensible mission statements, the question echoing through my head was, "What do these people *do* every day?"

If you think the DOE is atypical, replicate the exercise with any of the other cabinet agencies or large independent agencies. Leviathan by Proxy is real. But so is the Leviathan created by 2 million federal employees whose number John DiIulio wants to increase to 3 million.

I am sympathetic to many of DiIulio's recommendations and the reasoning behind them. But even if members of Congress were willing to pass the authorizing legislation, insurmountable objections stand in the way. In April 2014, the Partnership for Public Service and Booz Allen Hamilton published its analysis, *Building the Enterprise: A New Civil Service Framework.*[8] Its recommendations too were attractive in a purely theoretical sense. But the report also describes the reality of the current public service and how hard it is to attract good people.

As I have observed in my own encounters with the federal government, that reality starts with the dreariness of federal workplaces. In the private sector, corporate employers throughout the economy have transformed their offices into attractive, open spaces with bright colors, lots of light, and design tricks that encourage creative interaction among staff. If you go to work in an ordinary office of the federal government, you are still likely to be in a building with long halls lined with small, enclosed offices on either side. It is often drab and poorly maintained. Your computer and its software are likely to be antiquated even if they are critical to your job—the air traffic control system and the Internal Revenue Service are cases in point. Getting ordinary resources you need to do your job, down to routine office supplies, often requires permissions and delays inconceivable in the private sector.

Many of your coworkers have not been hired because of their qualifications and promise but to fill the many quotas that influence the federal hiring process. Once in their jobs, in the words of the authors of *Building the Enterprise*, "top performers seldom receive sufficient rewards, poor performers are rarely fired or demoted, and managers are not held accountable for how well they manage employees or the outcomes of the work they oversee."[9] People are routinely promoted a few steps beyond their level of competence. Again from *Building the Enterprise*: "Federal employee surveys routinely show that only about half of the workforce has a high level of respect for their senior leaders."[10] Even if you are promoted to a senior position, you find that you enjoy far less freedom to act than you would routinely get—indeed, be encouraged to exercise—in the private sector. Remuneration? It is the worst of both worlds: second-rate people in the federal bureaucracy make more than they could in the private sector; first-rate people make far less.

These realities of the federal workplace and civil service are not "mistakes" that the federal bureaucracy is eager to fix. They are built into the nature of the sclerotic state. The questions arise: Suppose we were to try to add a million people to the federal workforce. What kind of people would be attracted to them? Why would we have reason to expect them to perform any differently from those already in place?

But even these observations are irrelevant to predicting the future. Assume that none of them are true. The iron triangle of politicians seeking funds for reelection, bureaucratic managers protecting their own fiefdoms, and special interests plying the politicians with campaign contributions and the bureaucrats with prospects of going through the revolving door, creates a mutually reinforcing network of forces that will keep any of DiIulio's sensible reforms from coming to pass. This, too, is built into the nature of the sclerotic state.

A council of despair? Yes, for politics as usual. Olson mordantly observed that the best solution to the sclerotic state is to lose a catastrophic war, comparing the post–World War II economic fortunes of Germany and Japan with those of Britain and France. There are other solutions, however. They will come about by rebellion from without, not through reform conducted within today's political culture. But that's a topic for a book of its own.

Reply to E. J. Dionne Jr. and Charles Murray

‏≳≲‏

John J. DiIulio Jr.

I AM DEEPLY GRATEFUL for both the kind words and the constructively critical feedback provided by each of two major contemporary American thinkers about politics and government, E. J. Dionne Jr. and Charles Murray. Dionne is a proud liberal and Murray is a proud libertarian. Not surprisingly, the parts of the treatise that Dionne seems to like the most are the parts that Murray seems to like the least, and vice versa.

But, ideologically distinct though Dionne and Murray are from one another, my two interlocutors are as one in acknowledging that Washington's proxy-administration system is "out of hand" (Dionne) and "dysfunctional" (Murray). Let me try, however, to address their respective differences with each other—and with me—in ways that might help to clarify my case and maybe move all three of us closer together.

HOOKED ON LEV-PRO

Dionne agrees that we need a "wholesale reexamination of our habit of outsourcing." Without an "adequate number of employees," and without presidents that "take far more seriously the task of reforming and then running the operations of government," we won't "get the government we need for the things we want" (p. 116–117). If Congress ever gets serious about improving the federal government's performance, "DiIulio has provided them with a text to guide their reflections" (p. 121). And President Obama, tutored by the "experience of the HealthCare.gov website," should "read this book before he leaves office" and spark the revival of the "administrative presidency" for which it calls (p. 121).

But Dionne rejects what he takes to be my desire "to reduce the size of government." He eschews any implication that the government to gross domestic product (GDP) ratio is "a good measure of our freedom." He cites Medicare, Medicaid, and military spending and asks, "Are these threats to our freedom?" He acknowledges that one can't name ten people who have been without government funding of one type or another, but he demurs, "So what?" (pp. 117–118).

Dionne's "principal dissent" is to my use of the term "Leviathan." As he notes, the biblical Leviathan is a sea monster, and the Hobbesian Leviathan is an autocratic state. So, where does one who "has a passion for a government that works and for programs that succeed," who says "amen" to Dionne's own latest book in defense of a strong but limited national government,[1] and who is also an unrepentant Democrat[2] get off using the term "Leviathan" to "describe the current state of our constitutional republic"? (p. 121).

As someone who is infamous for coining and then regretting provocative terms ("Mayberry Machiavelli," "superpredator," and others), I am eager to avoid coining yet another term that I will shortly be regretting. But, in fact, the term I use to characterize, not our "constitutional republic," but our post-1960, ever-growing federal government, is not "Leviathan" but "Leviathan *by Proxy*," hereafter Lev-Pro.

Not, mind you, that using "Leviathan" all by itself to characterize our whale of a federal government would be wholly inappropriate, and not that doing so would be without respectable precedents. To cite just two:

- *A Hook in Leviathan: A Critical Interpretation of the Hoover Commission Report*, a 1950 volume coauthored by two of the day's leading former government officials, summarizing the midcentury commission's recommendations for reorganizing the federal bureaucracy (citing research by none other than the Brookings Institution).[3]
- "Taming Leviathan: A Special Report on the Future of the State," *The Economist*, a 2011 pull-out piece in that magazine's finest fact-based traditions.[4]

I may, in fact, be to Dionne's left in insisting that government has not just a civic duty but an absolute moral obligation to pursue what the Catholic Church calls "social justice" and to reduce what it calls "sinful inequalities."[5] Being allergic to government is as wrong-headed and wrong-hearted as being addicted to it. And amen to Dionne's dictum that the "test of a Leviathan state is not how big it is, but what it does."

But what Lev-Pro actually does is promise but not deliver on a huge range of federal programs. For instance, there are more than a half-dozen federal childhood antihunger laws on the books, yet "extreme food insecurity," as the U.S. Department of Agriculture (USDA) terms it, spikes each summer among low-income children. Why? Because, while black-letter federal law entitles poor kids to get USDA-funded summer meals, the actual participation rate nationally is below 15 percent.

And why's that? Lev-Pro, that's why.

In my hometown, Philadelphia, as of this writing, we have a great regional USDA office led by a veteran USDA civil servant who really cares about translating the feds' summer food entitlement promise into performance; a caring bunch of Pennsylvania Department of Education officials, including a former nurse-nutritionist, who constitute the USDA's primary Keystone State proxy; an incredible City Department of Recreation and Parks leader who cares lots about at-risk youth, and who has a staff to match and to serve as the program's primary local government proxy; an amazing cadre of four leaders (all women, by the way) in the Archdiocese of Philadelphia's Nutrition Development Services (NDS); and literally hundreds more individuals and institutions who partner with the state, the city, and NDS to supply nearly a million meals each summer to Philly kids who might otherwise just go hungry. (Witnessing how the kids at a summer USDA site bolt to the "food table" after a long weekend would break most hearts.)

Yet, for all that, Philly reaches only about 50 percent participation, making it one of the most "successful" big-city summer USDA antihunger sites in the nation. Lev-Pro yields far less in most other states and cities all across America. If I were to write a book about this one Lev-Pro federal program, I might entitle it "starving for bureaucracy." This is not "strong but limited" government. This is Lev-Pro, America's big intergovernment by proxy at its "best." It is just another illustration of the fact that, as I write in the body of this treatise, mid-twentieth-century liberals and their successors won "policy wars on poverty, on environmental protection, and on other issues without planning for the postwar administrative occupation."

Judged strictly by what it does, Lev-Pro, America's real big government, is as I described it: "hyperactive and anemic, overgrown and understaffed" (p. 92).

Thus, ask not whether Medicare or Medicaid is a threat to freedom and responsible citizenship. Rather, ask why millions of people receive program benefits without ever seeing a single government employee, and even believing that the benefits are not from the government at all ("Get government out of my Medicare!"). Ask also why each program is so financially challenged, unable to police improper payments, and implicated in America's spending far more of its GDP on health care, but having no better overall health care outcomes, than many other democratic nations do.

And as for whether military spending is a threat to freedom, ask President Eisenhower: the post-1960, single-bid military-industrial citadel is Lev-Pro on steroids, and the Lev-Pro-leveraged entitlement-nonprofit complex is not far behind it.

Dionne is absolutely right that, all by itself, government's share of GDP at any given point in time tells us nothing definitive about the state of freedom and democratic citizenship. But when that share rises from the twenties in the 1960s to the forties in the 2010s;[6] when government benefits make up about a fifth of Americans' income, and nearly half the citizenry lives in households that receive government benefits;[7] when more than 60 million people depend mainly on government for their health care, housing, and daily bread[8] (and when one truly can't name ten people who have not been supported by government to some nontrivial degree); when nonprofit sector leaders sound just like defense industry lobbyists in frothing about how decreases in government spending (or, more precisely, decreases in rates of government spending increases) will cost "private" but tax-funded jobs; and when government is run like a debt-financed, proxy-administered incumbent-protection racket, with laws that nobody actually reads authorizing programs that nobody can count or describe (let alone change and improve); then we must, I think, admit that Lev-Pro is a threat to freedom and to democratic citizenship, a gargantuan and grotesque form of big government, and a danger to the present and the future health of our "constitutional republic."

As Alexis de Tocqueville warned in 1840, a modern democratic nation can enervate freedom in the name of equality and degrade citizenship in insidious ways that no ancient tyrant's brute force or medieval aristocracy's brutish royals could; Lev-Pro looks to me too much like a twenty-first-century, all-American, pseudo-individualistic, and superficially antistatist version of the very "immense and tutelary power" about which Tocqueville warned.[9]

Lev-Pro's "administrative despotism" exercises power that is "absolute, minute, regular, provident, and mild."[10] It is less a "nanny state" than a "daddy state" in that it cultivates not liberty-loving, active, and even cantankerous democratic citizens (cantankerous enough to object to "nanny"), but passive dependents and petty supplicants (always ready to resent but make room for "daddy").[11] It only requires that "the people shake off their dependence just long enough" to reelect their tax less/spend more incumbent leaders (low voter turnout rates are just what the Lev-Pro state's leaders in both parties want) and then quickly "relapse into it again"[12] by demanding more, more, more debt-financed, posterity-be-damned benefits, and seeking more, more, more Lev-Pro-bestowed subsidies, loans, grants and contracts.

RX FOR DEMOSCLEROSIS

In contradistinction to Dionne, Murray's principal worry is that I am, if anything, too sanguine about "Leviathan," not least regarding my—in his view, misguided—proposal to hire a million more federal bureaucrats by 2035. Murray does not cite his own plan "to replace the welfare state" (as I intimated in my treatise, the most thoughtful and forthright such plan yet proposed by any conservative thinker, despite its political infeasibility) but, instead, invokes the works of Mancur Olson and argues that the "federal government has reached an advanced stage of sclerosis."[13] *Bring Back the Bureaucrats*, he avers, reads "like case studies of Olson's theory in practice," illustrating the fed-led "hardening of the arteries and nerves of the body politic" (p. 125). He also cites Jonathan Rauch's 1999 book, *Government's End: Why Washington Stopped Working*.[14]

Murray agrees that "the core functions" of "the administrative state" should be "administered by full-time federal employees," but believes that these core functions "have been swamped by others that range from the silly to the destructive" (pp. 125–26).

Murray characterizes federal bureaucrats as quite a sorry lot: ill-trained, "second-rate people" who, to "fill the many quotas" that govern the federal personnel hiring process, are "routinely promoted a few steps beyond their level of competence;" they work in "often drab and poorly maintained" offices (nothing like the private sector's "attractive, open spaces with bright colors, lots of light" and room for "creative interaction among staff"), and yet get paid "more than they could" command "in the private sector" (pp. 128–29.)

Murray concludes with a virtual "counsel of despair": reelection-seeking incumbents, special interests, and bureaucrats "with prospects of going through the revolving door" create a "mutually reinforcing network of forces that will keep any of DiIulio's sensible reforms from coming to pass" (p. 130) He judges my least sensible proposal to be my call for hiring more federal bureaucrats.

I cannot but share certain parts of Murray's despair about trimming, taming, and improving Lev-Pro. The book by Rauch that he cites was actually a revised version of his 1994 treatise, *Demosclerosis: The Silent Killer of American Government.*[15] But in light of four considerations, I would appeal to Murray to consider again whether hiring more federal bureaucrats could cauterize if not cure, slow if not stop, America's political, administrative, and civic "demosclerosis"—and maybe even make the federal government work better, achieve more, and cost less.

First, James Q. Wilson (among others) has cast serious

doubts on how useful Olson's concepts and theories truly are to explaining and predicting what political organizations and government bureaucracies do and how they do it,[16] and R. Douglas Arnold has used these same theories to explore how Congress does, under certain conditions, transcend "politics as usual" and produce "general interest legislation."[17]

Second, what Theodore J. Lowi termed "interest-group liberalism"[18] is, in the age of Lev-Pro, more like "implementation-group liberalism": Washington is beset by proxies' lobbies both at the front end of the lawmaking process and at the back end of the administrative execution and oversight process; as I write in the treatise, "they hardly ever lose—which is why government never stops growing" (p. 28). Pruning proxies is thus the necessary but insufficient condition for changing the politics of federal policymaking in ways that make trimming and taming Lev-Pro possible. Since there is no real public appetite for real cuts in most federal programs, a slow but steady shift from proxy administration to direct public administration (more full-time federal bureaucrats, fewer proxies) might help to gradually reduce the political pressures favoring incessant government growth.

Third, I can assure Murray that most federal bureaucrats are far (far!) better on all counts than he seems to think they are, including many who behave as what I have elsewhere described as "principled agents."[19] And I can vouch that many, though by no means most, federal workplaces are now almost as open, bright, and otherwise well-appointed as the finest private sector workplaces. Still, Murray's description of the plight of the federal civil service is by no means without factual foundations. In 1996, long before the latest reports on the subject, Donald F. Kettl, as usual, nailed the troubled truth about the need for civil service reform, including how the "current civil service system struggles to produce and retain the skilled professionals government needs to perform its work," and how it "does not adequately motivate government employees to high performance," among other serious, long-standing problems.[20]

Fourth and finally, the central finding of Kettl's review of the civil service system was as follows:

> The current civil service system has become a politically useful whipping boy for public management problems rooted in the federal government's system of governance. . . . The number of federal employees, in fact, has remained remarkably steady since the mid-1950s. . . . If there is a "big government" problem, it is not a problem caused by or rooted in the number of government employees. The real growth of government has come through an expansion of grants, contracts, and, especially, entitlements.[21]

As I stress in this treatise, Lev-Pro is first and foremost the creature of the incumbent-dominated Congress. Behind all those reports about federal program "duplication" and "overlap" and "waste" are not incompetent bureaucrats exercising renegade discretion, but lousy lawmakers and diverse sets of politically entrenched proxies, each of which gets to wet its beak and get its funding without regard to the most rudimentary principles of cost-effective public administration. Nobody who wanted to translate good laws into good administrative actions, and who was the least bit sane, would design Lev-Pro from scratch.

So, on at least this much, I hope that liberals, libertarians, and all citizens everywhere might agree: having ever fewer people handling ever more public money, doing ever more (and ever more complicated) tasks, and managing ever expanding legions of proxies is a recipe for the very past administrative disasters that the federal government has experienced as well as a guarantee of more—and worse—disasters to come, unless and until we not only hire more full-time federal workers but train, motivate, performance manage, and reward them as if our public well-being depended on it.

It does.

Notes

ACKNOWLEDGMENTS

1. John J. DiIulio Jr., "Principled Agents: The Cultural Bases of Behavior in a Federal Government Bureaucracy," *Journal of Public Administration Research and Theory* 4, no. 3 (1994): 277–317.
2. Gerald J. Garvey, *Facing the Bureaucracy: Living and Dying in a Public Agency* (San Francisco: Jossey Bass, 1993), and *Public Administration: Profession and Practice—A Case Study Approach* (New York: St. Martin's Press, 1996).
3. John J. DiIulio Jr., "Facing Up to Big Government," *National Affairs* no. 1 (Spring 2012): 22–41.

INTRODUCTION

1. Alexander Hamilton, "Federalist No. 1," in *The Federalist Papers*, ed. Clinton Rossiter (New York: Signet, 1961), 33.
2. Obamacare is just one recent, major, and much-publicized example; see the reports on its early implementation by more than sixty researchers across thirty-five states on the website of the Rockefeller Institute of Government (http://www.rockinst.org).
3. *U.S. House of Representatives Subcommittee on Federal Workforce, U.S. Postal Service and Labor Policy: Hearing on Rightsizing the Federal Workforce*, 112th Cong. 11 (May 26, 2011) (statement of U.S. Representative Cynthia Lummins).

4. The National Commission on Fiscal Responsibility and Reform, *The Moment of Truth: Report of the National Commission on Fiscal Responsibility and Reform* (Washington, DC: The White House, December 1, 2010), 1.10.4.

5. Ibid.

6. James Madison, "Federalist No. 14," in Rossiter, *The Federalist Papers*, 104.

7. Alexander Hamilton, "Federalist No. 70," in Rossiter, *The Federalist Papers*, 423.

CHAPTER 1

1. *Annual Report of the Boards of Trustees of the Federal Hospital Insurance and Federal Supplemental Medical Insurance Trust Funds* (Washington, DC, 2013), 228–29 and appendix G. The 2012 report projected that the Medicare trust fund could be exhausted by or before 2024 (28), and that certain recent changes in federal law could spell even worse financial stress for the program than projected (278).

2. On Bureaucrats, 1960–2013, see the following: U.S. Office of Personnel Management (opm.gov), Federal Employment Reports, Historical Workforce Tables Since 1940, Executive Branch Civilian Employment, and *Sizing Up the Executive Branch Fiscal Year 2013* (Washington, DC, 2014); U.S. Office of Management and Budget (omb.gov), Historical Tables, Total Executive Branch Civilian Full-Time Equivalent (FTE), 1981–2015, table 17.1; Partnership for Public Service and Booz Allen Hamilton, *Building the Enterprise: A New Civil Service Framework*, (Washington, DC, April 2014), 1; and U.S. Congressional Budget Office, *Federal Civilian Employment: A Special Study* (Washington, DC, December 1987). On Budgets, 1960–2013, see U.S. Office of Management and Budget (omb.gov), Historical Tables, Summary of Receipts, Outlays, and Surpluses or Deficits, table 1.1 (with annual outlays data adapted by author to reflect constant 2013 dollars).

3. U.S. Congressional Budget Office, *Federal Grants to State and Local Governments* (Washington, DC, March 2013), 6; also see U.S. Government Accountability Office, *Grants to State and Local Governments: An Overview of Federal Funding Levels and Selected Challenges* (Washington, DC, September 2012).

4. White House, *Economic Report of the President, Transmitted to the Congress March 2013 Together with the Annual Report of the Council of Economic Advisers* (Washington, DC, March 2013), 114, figure 3-13, shows that in constant 2005 dollars total federal grants to state and local governments rose from $45.3 billion in 1960 to $504.4 billion in 2012.

5. U.S. Census Bureau, *Annual Survey of Public Employment and Payroll Summary Report: 2011* (Washington, DC, August 22, 2013), 2.

6. Ibid., 5, 10.

7. U.S. Senate, Health, Education, Labor, and Pensions Committee, *Majority Committee Staff Report: Acting Responsibly? Federal Contractors Frequently Put Workers' Lives and Livelihoods at Risk* (Washington, DC, December 11, 2013), 1; U.S. Government Accountability Office, *Interagency Contracting: Agency Lessons Address Key Management Challenges, but Additional Steps Needed to Ensure Consistent Implementation of Policy Changes* (Washington, DC, January 2013), 1.

8. U.S. Government Accountability Office, *Human Capital: Additional Steps Needed to Help Determine the Right Size and Composition of DOD's Total Workforce* (Washington, DC, May 2013), and *Defense Contracting: Actions Needed to Increase Competition* (Washington, DC, March 2013).

9. U.S. Department of Health and Human Services (HHS), *Fiscal Year 2013 Agency Financial Report* (Washington, DC, December 2013); HHS Office of the Inspector General, *Protecting HHS Grant and Contracts Funds from Fraud, Waste, and Abuse: Management Challenge 9* (Washington, DC, 2013); *U.S. Senate Homeland Security and Government Affairs Committee, Subcommittee on Federal Financial Management, Government Information, Federal Service, and International Security*, 112th Cong. (July 25, 2012) (statement of Nancy J. Gunderson).

10. U.S. Senate, *Majority Committee Staff Report: Acting Responsibly?* 1.

11. Sarah L. Pettijohn, *The Nonprofit Sector in Brief: Public Charities, Giving, and Volunteering* (Washington, DC: Urban Institute, 2013), 2; see also Molly F. Sherlock and James G. Ravelle, *An Overview of the Nonprofit and Charitable Sector* (Washington, DC: Congressional Research Service, November 17, 2009), 3, 16.

12. Sarah L. Pettijohn et al., *Nonprofit-Government Contracts and Grants:*

Findings from the 2013 National Survey (Washington, DC: Urban Institute, December 2013), 1.

13. U.S. Government Accountability Office, *Grants Management: Oversight of Selective States' Disbursement of Federal Funds Addresses Timeliness and Administrative Allowances* (Washington, DC, April 2013), 1.

14. Lester M. Salamon et al., *Nonprofit Employment Bulletin: No. 39, The Johns Hopkins Nonprofit Economic Data Project* (Baltimore: Johns Hopkins University, 2012), 2.

15. Sherlock and Ravelle, *An Overview*, 16, notes also that some nonprofit organizations issue tax-exempt bonds.

16. John J. DiIulio Jr., *Godly Republic: A Centrist Blueprint for America's Faith-Based Future* (Berkeley: University of California Press, 2007).

17. U.S. Office of Management and Budget, *Budget of the United States Fiscal Year 2013*, 137–38, table 6.1 (author-calculated average of 2009–2013 federal outlays as a percentage of gross domestic product data).

18. Benjamin Zycher, *State and Local Spending: Do Tax and Expenditure Limits Work?* (Washington, DC: American Enterprise Institute, May 2013), 6–7, table 1.

19. John Micklethwait, "Taming Leviathan: A Special Report on the Future of the State," *The Economist*, March 19, 2011, 4.

20. Manhattan Institute, *The U.S. and Europe: Governments of Equal Size?* (New York: Manhattan Institute, February 28, 2012), 1, reporting World Economic Outlook data from the International Monetary Fund.

21. Daniel Harper, "U.S. Per Person Debt Now Higher Than That of Greece," *Weekly Standard*, November 5, 2012, 1, reporting data based on estimates by the International Monetary Fund; see also $52,888 per capita federal debt estimate for 2013 and $19,238 total government spending estimate for 2013, at http://www.usgovernmentspending .com/year_spending2013USdn_15ds2n, accessed April 7, 2014. I do not include state and local government debt because many experts on subnational government and public finance believe that aggregating the data across fifty states and tens of thousands of local jurisdictions yields questionable estimates.

22. International Monetary Fund, *World Economic Outlook: Outlook 2012—Coping with High Debt and Sluggish Growth* (Washington,

DC: International Monetary Fund, October 2012), 101, table 2; Mick-lethwait, "Taming Leviathan," 5.

23. Bill Allison, "Good Enough for Government Work? The Contractors Building Obamacare," last modified October 14, 2013, accessed October 15, 2013, http://www.philly.com, reporting on data gathered by the Sunlight Foundation.

24. Health and Human Services, *Protecting HHS Grant and Contracts*.

25. Ed O'Keefe, "Eye Opener: Homeland Security Has More Contractors than Feds," *Washington Post*, February 24, 2010, http://voices.washington post.com/federal-eye/2010/02/eye_opener_homeland_security_h_h.

26. Dana Priest and William M. Arkin, "A Hidden World, Growing Beyond Control" and "National Security Inc," *Washington Post*, July 19–21, 2010. Also see Dana Hedgpeth, "Congress Says DHS Oversaw $15 Billion in Failed Contracts," *Washington Post*, September 17, 2008.

27. Emma Ellman-Golan, "No Hungry Summer for Philadelphia Children," *Philadelphia Daily News*, June 21, 2011. The report on the U.S. Department of Agriculture program referenced in the article is available at http://www.foxleadership.upenn.edu.

28. U.S. Government Accountability Office, *Superfund: EPA Should Take Steps to Improve Its Management of Alternatives to Placing Sites on the National Priorities List* (Washington, DC, April 2013).

29. U.S. Government Accountability Office, *Department of Energy: Observations on DOE's Management Challenges and Steps Taken to Address Them, Statement of David C. Trimble, Director of Natural Resources and Environment* (Washington, DC, July 24, 2013), 4.

30. Frank Thompson and John J. DiIulio Jr., eds., *Medicaid and Devolution* (Washington, DC: Brookings Institution Press, 1998); see also American Health Care Association, *A Report on Shortfalls in Medicaid Funding for Nursing Center Care* (ELJAY LLC, December 2012), esti-mating that in 2012 Medicaid underfunded nursing care centers by $7 billion.

31. U.S. Government Accountability Office, *Additional Opportunities to Reduce Fragmentation, Overlap, and Duplication and Achieve Other Financial Benefits* (Washington, DC, April 2014) and U.S. Government Accountability Office, *Government Efficiency and Effectiveness: Strategies for Reducing Fragmentation, Overlap, and Duplication and Achieving Cost Savings, Statement of Gene L. Dodaro,*

Comptroller General of the United States (Washington, DC, May 16, 2013).

32. U.S. Government Accountability Office, *Improper Payments: Recent Efforts to Address Improper Payments and Recovery Challenges* (Washington, DC, April 2011), GAO Overview Page.

33. U.S. Government Accountability Office, *Health Care Fraud: Indicators Provide Information on Program Accomplishments, but Assessing Program Effectiveness Is Difficult* (Washington, DC, September 2013) and U.S. Government Accountability Office, *Medicare Program Integrity: Increasing Consistency of Contractor Requirements May Improve Administrative Efficiency* (Washington, DC, July 2013).

34. Anne M. Khademian, "Hurricane Katrina and the Failure of Homeland Security," in *Judging Bush*, ed. Robert Maranto et al. (Redwood City, CA: Stanford University Press, 2009); Ronald J. Daniels et al., eds., *On Risk and Disaster: Lessons from Hurricane Katrina* (Philadelphia: University of Pennsylvania Press, 2006).

35. Eric J. Chaisson, *The Hubble Wars: Astrophysics Meets Astropolitics in the Two-Billion-Dollar Struggle Over the Hubble Space Telescope* (Cambridge, MA: Harvard University Press, 1998).

36. U.S. Government Accountability Office, *Housing and Urban Development: Strategic Human Capital and Workforce Planning Should be an Ongoing Priority* (Washington, DC, March 2013) and Debbie Cenziper and Jonathan Mummolo, "A Trail of Stalled or Abandoned HUD Projects," *Washington Post*, May 14, 2011.

37. U.S. Government Accountability Office, *VA Health Care: Additional Guidance, Training, and Oversight Needed to Improve Clinical Contract Monitoring* (Washington, DC, October 2013).

38. U.S. Government Accountability Office, *Defense Contracting: Actions Needed to Increase Competition* (Washington, DC, March 2013).

39. U.S. Government Accountability Office, *Acquisition Workforce: DOT Lacks Data, Oversight, and Strategic Focus Needed to Address Workforce Challenges* (Washington, DC, January 2013).

40. U.S. Government Accountability Office, *Superfund: EPA Should Take Steps to Improve Its Management of Alternatives to Placing Sites on the National Priorities List* (Washington, DC, April 2013).

41. U.S. Government Accountability Office, *Tax Gap: IRS Could Significantly Increase Revenues by Better Targeting Enforcement Resources*

(Washington, DC, December 2012); see also Tony Pugh, "Unpaid Taxes Total $400 Billion, But Little Political Will to Pursue It," *Seattle Times*, July 3, 2011, http://seattletimes.nwsource.com/html/nationworld/2015503714_taxgap04.html.

42. U.S. Government Accountability Office, *Contract Management: Guidance Needed for Using Performance-Based Service Contracting* (Washington, DC, September 2002), and U.S. Government Accountability Office, *Executive Branch Should More Fully Employ the GPRA Modernization Act to Address Governance Challenges* (Washington, DC, June 2013).

43. John J. DiIulio Jr., and Richard P. Nathan, eds., *Making Health Reform Work: The View from the States* (Washington, DC: Brookings Institution Press, 1994).

44. Rockefeller Institute–Fels Institute 2014 reports on "Managing Health Care Reform: Implementation of the Affordable Care Act," at http://www.rockinst.org; see also Fels Institute of Government, "Beyond the Website: A Study of the Early Implementation of the Affordable Care Act in Pennsylvania," February 2, 2014, http://www.fels.upenn.edu/ACA.

45. James Madison, "Federalist No. 10," in *The Federalist Papers*, ed. Clinton Rossiter (New York: Signet, 1961), 77.

46. Allison, "Good Enough for Government Work"; see also Staff of the *Washington Post*, *Landmark: The Inside Story of America's New Health Care Law and What It Means For Us All* (New York: Public Affairs, 2010).

47. Marion Blakey, president and CEO, American Aerospace Industries (National Press Club, Washington, DC, September 14, 2011).

48. Diana Aviv, president and CEO, to Independent Sector mailing list, November 10, 2011, "Pennsylvania Advocates: Act Now to Preserve the Charitable Deduction."

49. Diana Aviv, president and CEO, to Independent Sector mailing list, November 20, 2011, "Tick. Tick. Tick."

CHAPTER 2

1. Rasmussen Reports, "24% Trust Federal Government to Do Right Thing Most or All the Time" (poll, June 13, 2013, poll conducted June

10–13, 2013). In 2011, public distrust peaked at 89 percent; see Jeff Zeleny, "New Poll Finds a Deep Distrust of Government," *New York Times*, October 26, 2011, reporting data from a *New York Times*/CBS News poll.

2. Gallup, "Congress Approval Stagnant at Low Level" (poll, March 13, 2013, poll conducted March 7–10, 2013).

3. Pew Research Center, "Majority Says the Federal Government Threatens Their Personal Rights" (poll, January 31, 2013, poll conducted January 9–13, 2013).

4. Anderson Roberts Research and Shaw & Company Research, Fox News Poll (poll, August 23, 2012, poll conducted August 19–21, 2012).

5. Office of U.S. Congressman Paul Ryan, "Wyden and Ryan Advance Bipartisan Plan to Strengthen Medicare and Expand Health Care Choices for All," December 15, 2011, 2–3, http://paulryan.house.gov/news/documentsingle.aspx?DocumentID=272682. See also AARP, "AARP Members Send Millions of Petitions to Congress—Seniors Want Washington to Oppose Any Budget Deal That Cuts Social Security and Medicare Benefits" (press release, November 15, 2011).

6. James Q. Wilson et al., *American Government: Institutions and Policies*, 14th ed. (Boston: Cengage Learning, 2014), 313.

7. Ibid.

8. Ibid., 313–14.

9. Douglas L. Kriner and Andrew Reeves, "The Influence of Federal Spending on Presidential Elections," *American Political Science Review* 106, no. 2 (May 2012): 348–66.

10. James Q. Wilson, *Bureaucracy: What Government Agencies Do and Why They Do It* (New York: Basic Books, 1989), 236.

11. Ibid.

12. Ibid., 251.

13. Ibid.

14. Martha Derthick, *Keeping the Compound Republic: Essays on American Federalism* (Washington, DC: Brookings Institution Press, 2001), 63.

15. Theodore J. Lowi, *The End of Liberalism: The Second Republic of the United States* (New York: W. W. Norton, 1969).

16. Ibid., 298.

17. Ibid.

18. Wilson, *American Government*, 255.

19. Lee Jared Drutman, "The Business of America Is Lobbying: The Expansion of Corporate Activity and the Future Is American Pluralism," (PhD dissertation, University of California, Berkeley, Fall 2010); Kay Lehrman Schlozman et al., "Who Sings in the Heavenly Chorus? The Shape of Organized Interest Group Activity" (paper presented at the Annual Meeting of the American Political Science Association, Boston, MA, August 2008).

20. James Q. Wilson, "The Bureaucracy Problem," *The Public Interest* no. 6 (Winter 1967).

21. James Q. Wilson, *Political Organizations* (New York: Basic Books, 1973), chapter 16, and James Q. Wilson, *The Politics of Regulation* (New York: Basic Books, 1980), 367–72; Theodore J. Lowi, "American Business, Public Policy, Case-Studies, and Theory," *World Politics* 16, no. 4 (July 1964).

22. John W. Kingdon, *Agendas, Alternatives, and Public Policies* (New York: Little, Brown, 1984); Nelson Polsby, *Political Innovation in America: The Politics of Policy Initiation* (New Haven, CT: Yale University Press, 1985).

23. U.S. Government Accountability Office, *Recovery Act: Grant Implementation Experiences Offer Lessons for Accountability and Transparency* (Washington, DC, June 2014); U.S. Government Accountability Office, *Recovery Act: Thousands of Recovery Act Contract and Grant Recipients Owe Millions in Federal Taxes* (Washington, DC, April 2011); U.S. General Accountability Office, *Recovery Act: Opportunities to Improve Management and Strengthen Accountability Over States' and Localities' Uses of Funds* (Washington, DC, September 2010).

24. Donald F. Kettl, *The Next Government of the United States: Why Our Institutions Fail Us and How to Fix Them* (New York: W. W. Norton, 2009), 10.

25. Ibid., 6, emphasis in the original.

26. Ibid., 11–12.

27. Ibid., 12.

28. Patricia Barry, "New to Medicare?" *AARP Bulletin*, November 2013, 30.

29. Ibid., 34.

30. Organization for Economic Co-operation and Development, "Health Policies and Data: Health Spending Continues to Stagnate, OECD Says," June 27, 2013, http://www.oecd.org/newsroom/health-spending -continues-to-stagnate-says-oecd.htm.

31. Ibid.

32. See reports starting in January 2014, Center for Medicare and Medicaid Services (http://www.cms.gov).

33. OECD, "Health Spending Continues to Stagnate, OECD Says," June 27, 2013, http://www.oecd.org/newsroom/health-spending-continues -to-stagnate-says-oecd.htm.

34. Patricia Barry, "New to Medicare?" 34.

35. U.S. Environmental Protection Agency. "Budget and Workforce Data, 1970-2013." Accessed January 3, 2014. http://www2.epa.gov/ planandbudget/budget.

36. U.S. Environmental Protection Agency, *FY 2013: EPA Budget in Brief, EPA's FTE Ceiling History* (Washington, DC, 2013), 11.

37. Ibid.

38. U.S. Government Accountability Office, *Environmental Protection: EPA's Progress in Closing Completed Grants and Contracts* (Washington, DC, November 11, 1998).

39. USA Spending. "Prime Award Spending Data, Environmental Protection Agency." Accessed January 3, 2014. http://www.usaspending.gov/ explore?&carryfilters=on &tab=By%20Agency&fiscal_year=2; U.S. Environmental Protection Agency, *FY 2013: EPA Budget in Brief*.

40. For the latest list of the EPA's "Green Power Partnership: Top 30 Local Government," visit http://www.epa.gov/greenpower/toplists/top30lo calgov.htm

41. Environmental Council of the States, *The State Environmental Agencies' Statement of Need and Budget Proposal for EPA's 2012 Categorical Grants STAG Budget (State and Tribal Assistance Grants)* (Washington, DC, June 2010), 1; see also Environmental Council on the States Green Report, *State Environmental Expenditures, 2005–2008* (Washington, DC, March 2008).

42. John J. DiIulio Jr. et al., *Improving Government Performance: An Owner's Manual* (Washington, DC: Brookings Institution Press, 1993), 34.

43. Gerald J. Garvey et al., "An Ounce of Implementation," in *Making Health Reform Work: The View from the States* ed. John J. DiIulio Jr. and Richard P. Nathan (Washington, DC: Brookings Institution Press, 1994), 139.

44. David Vogel, *National Styles of Regulation* (Ithaca, NY: Cornell University Press, 1986), 19–30.

45. U.S. Government Accountability Office, *Superfund: EPA Should Take Steps to Improve Its Management of Alternatives to Placing Sites on the National Priorities List* (Washington, DC, April 2013), 1.

46. Ibid., 16.

47. Ibid., 13, 36.

48. Ibid, 19, 36.

49. U.S. Government Accountability Office, *Pesticides: EPA Should Take Steps to Improve Its Oversight of Conditional Registrations* (Washington, DC, August 2013), 1.

50. Ibid., 23.

51. Ibid.

52. Ibid., 32.

53. Pew Research Center for the People and the Press, "Wide Partisan Differences on Global Warming" (Washington, DC, October 27, 2010).

54. National Center for Veterans Analysis and Statistics, *Statistics at a Glance* (Washington, DC, July 2013); U.S. Department of Veterans Affairs, *Strategic Plan Refresh: FY 2011–2015* (Washington, DC, 2011).

55. Ibid.

56. U.S. Department of Veterans Affairs, Office of Acquisitions and Logistics, "Doing Business with VA." Accessed January 4, 2014. http://www.va.gov/oal/business/dbwva.asp.

57. "Upcoming Audio Conference: Finding Funds for Veterans and Their Families," *Federal and Foundation Assistance Monitor*, October 25, 2013.

58. U.S. Government Accountability Office, *VA Health Care*, GAO Overview Page.

59. Ibid.

CHAPTER 3

1. U.S. Government Accountability Office, *Managing for Results: Executive Branch Should More Fully Implement the GPRA Modernization Act to Address Pressing Governance Challenges* (Washington, DC, June 2013), GAO Overview Page.

2. U.S. Government Accountability Office, *Additional Opportunities to Reduce Fragmentation, Overlap, and Duplication and Achieve Other Financial Benefits* (Washington, DC, April 8, 2014), and U.S. Government Accountability Office, *Government Efficiency and Effectiveness: Strategies for Reducing Fragmentation, Overlap, and Duplication and Achieving Cost Savings, Statement of Gene L. Dodaro, Comptroller General of the United States* (Washington, DC, May 16, 2013).

3. U.S. Government Accountability Office, *Managing for Results*, 2.

4. U.S. General Accountability Office, *Additional Opportunities to Reduce Fragmentation*, and Gregory Korte, "Government Often Has 10 Agencies Doing One Job," *USA Today*, April 8, 2014, 4A.

5. U.S. Government Accountability Office, *Interagency Contracting: Agency Actions Address Key Management Challenges, but Additional Steps Needed to Ensure Consistent Implementation of Policy Changes* (Washington, DC, January 2013).

6. For example, see U.S. Government Accountability Office, *Child Welfare: States Use Flexible Funds, But Struggle to Meet Service Needs* (Washington, DC, January 2013), reporting that states use funds under Title IV-B of the Social Security Act in myriad ways according to "different strategies for spending these funds" (1), that some states blend those Title IV-B child welfare program funds with other federal funds from other federal programs (Temporary Assistance for Needy Families, Social Services Block Grant, and Medicaid) (1), and that some states have been granted waivers that permit them to use funds from other federal programs to fund services (e.g., parenting classes and substance abuse treatment) in conjunction with Title IV-B child welfare program (20).

7. U.S. Government Accountability Office, *Oversight of Selected States' Disbursement of Federal Funds*, 6.

8. U.S. Government Accountability Office, *Executive Branch Should*

More Fully Employ the GPRA Modernization Act to Address Governance Challenges (Washington, DC, June 2013), 13.

9. U.S. Government Accountability Office, *Budget Issues: FEMA Needs Adequate Data, Plans, and Systems to Effectively Manage Resources for Day-to-Day Operations* (Washington, DC, January 19, 2007), 7, 22.

10. Ibid., GAO Overview Page.

11. Ibid., 5.

12. Ibid., 6.

13. Ibid., 14.

14. Ibid., 7.

15. U.S. Federal Emergency Management Agency, *2012 The State of FEMA* (Washington, D.C., 2012), 2.

16. U.S. Government Accountability Office, *FEMA Reservists: Training Could Benefit from Examination of Practices at Other Agencies* (Washington, DC, April 22, 2013), 1.

17. Ibid., 1, 4.

18. U.S. Government Accountability Office, *Social Security Administration: Long-Term Strategy Needed to Address Key Management Challenges* (Washington, DC, May 2013), 2–5, 7.

19. Ibid., 7.

20. Ibid, 1.

21. Ibid., 3–4.

22. Ibid., 8.

23. Ibid.

24. Ibid.

25. Ibid., 21.

26. Ibid., 10.

27. Ibid., 34.

28. Commissioner Charles O. Rossotti, *Report to the IRS Board Assessment of the IRS and the Tax System* (Washington, DC, September 2002), 1–2.

29. Ibid., 12–13.

30. Treasury Inspector General for Tax Administration, *Improvements Have Been Made to Address Human Capital Issues, but Continued Focus Is Needed* (Washington, DC, January 11, 2013).

31. Ibid.

32. U.S. General Accounting Office, *Report to the Commissioner of Internal Revenue: Administrative Changes Could Strengthen IRS' Claims for Rewards Program* (Washington, DC, April 19, 1985), 1. (Note: The General Accounting Office is today the Government Accountability Office).

33. U.S. Government Accountability Office, *Tax Gap: IRS Could Significantly Increase Revenues by Better Targeting Enforcement Resources* (Washington, DC, December 2012), 3.

34. Ibid.

35. Ibid., 8.

36. Sarah L. Pettijohn et al., *Nonprofit-Government Contracts and Grants: Findings from the 2013 National Survey* (Washington, DC: Urban Institute, December 2013), 2.

37. U.S. Government Accountability Office, *Human Capital: Additional Steps Needed to Help Determine the Right Size and Composition of DOD's Total Workforce* (Washington, DC, May 2013), and U.S. Government Accountability Office, *Defense Contracting: Actions Needed to Increase Competition* (Washington, DC, March 2013), 2.

38. Walter Pincus, "F-35 Production a Troubling Example of Pentagon Spending," *Washington Post*, December 26, 2011; Elisabeth Bumiller and Thomas Shanker, "Panetta to Offer Strategy for Cutting Military Budget," *New York Times*, January 4, 2012; Robert Burns, "U.S. Committed to F-35, Panetta Says," Associated Press, January 21, 2012, accessed January 21, 2012, http://www.philly.com.

39. U.S. Government Accountability Office, *Contractor Performance: DOD Actions to Improve the Reporting of Past Performance Information* (Washington, DC, June 2013).

40. U.S. Government Accountability Office, *Department of Energy: Observations on DOE's Management Challenges and Steps Taken to Address Them* (Washington, DC, July 2013); GovExec .com, "Top 25 Energy Department Contractors." Accessed January 8, 2014. http://www.govexec.com/magazine/2010/08/top-25-energy -department-contractors/32157/.

41. U.S. Department of Energy. "Staff and Contractors." Accessed January 8, 2014. http://energy.gov/about-us/staff-and-contractors.

42. Ibid., 8.

43. Ibid., 9.

44. U.S. Government Accountability Office, *Acquisition Workforce: DOT Lacks Data, Oversight, and Strategic Focus Needed to Address Significant Workforce Challenges* (Washington, DC, January 2013).

45. Ibid., GAO Overview Page.

46. U.S. Government Accountability Office, *Health Care Fraud and Abuse Control Program: Indicators Provide Information on Program Accomplishments, but Assessing Program Effectiveness Is Difficult* (Washington, DC, September 2013), 9.

47. Ibid., 22.

48. U.S. Government Accountability Office, *Medicare Program Integrity: Increasing Consistency of Contractor Requirements May Improve Administrative Efficiency* (Washington, DC, July 2013), 1.

49. Ibid., 4.

50. Ibid., 19.

51. U.S. Department of Health and Human Services, *Fiscal Year 2013 Agency Financial Report* (Washington, DC, December 2013), 15, showing that improper payments have actually inched up in recent years.

52. Stuart Butler, "Commentary on Privatization: Forms, Limits, and Relations to a Positive Theory of Government," *Marquette Law Review* 71 (1988): 526.

53. E. S. Savas, *Privatization: The Key to Better Government* (Chatham, NJ: Chatham House, 1987).

54. James Q. Wilson, *Bureaucracy: What Government Agencies Do and Why They Do It* (New York: Basic Books, 1989), 350. Then as now, I harbor more doubts than Wilson did about the relative advantages of for-profit prisons; see John J. DiIulio Jr., "The Duty to Govern: A Critical Perspective on the Private Management of Prisons and Jails," in *Private Prisons and the Public Interest*, ed. Douglas C. McDonald (New Brunswick, NJ: Rutgers University Press, 1990), 155–78.

55. Steve Kelman, *Procurement and Public Management: The Fear of Discretion and the Quality of Government Performance* (Washington, DC: AEI Press, 1990), and Steve Kelman, "Deregulating Federal Procurement: Nothing to Fear But Discretion Itself," in *Deregulating*

the Public Service: Can Government Be Improved? ed. John J. DiIulio Jr. (Washington, DC: Brookings Institution Press, 1994), chapter 6, especially 108–15.

56. Steve Kelman, "A New Way to Use Past Performance in Contracting," July 9, 2012, http://fcw.com/blogs/lectern/2012/07/past-performance-future-results.aspx.

57. Nicholas Henry, "Federal Contracting: Government's Dependency on Private Contractors," in *The State of Public Administration: Issues, Challenge, and Opportunities*, eds. Donald C. Menzel and Harvey L. White (Armonk, NY: M.E. Sharpe, 2011), 226.

58. U.S. Government Accountability Office, *Defense Contracting: Actions Needed to Increase Competition* (Washington, DC, March 2013).

59. Sarah Pettijohn et al., *Nonprofit-Government Contracts and Grants*, 9–10.

60. Ibid., 10.

61. Ram A. Cnaan, *The Other Philadelphia Story: How Local Congregations Support Quality of Life in Urban America* (Philadelphia: University of Pennsylvania Press, 2006); Ram A. Cnaan, *The Invisible Caring Hand: American Congregations and the Provision of Welfare* (New York: New York University Press, 2002), and Ram A. Cnaan, *The Newer Deal: Social Work and Religion in Partnership* (New York: Columbia University Press, 1999).

62. John J. DiIulio Jr., *Godly Republic: A Centrist Blueprint for America's Faith-Based Future* (Berkeley: University of California Press, 2007).

63. Butler, "Commentary on Privatization," 531.

64. Ibid., 526, 531. It is also worth noting that Butler (see 532) also warned that even "privatization" via "vouchers" could "invite government regulation" of the voucher-paid nongovernmental organizations and "actually extend the power and domain of government, rather than reduce it."

65. Nicholas Henry, "Federal Contracting," chapter 14, 229, 234.

66. Project on Government Oversight, *Bad Business: Billions of Taxpayer Dollars Wasted on Hiring Contractors* (Washington, DC, September 13, 2011), 1.

67. Ibid., 2, citing Paul C. Light, *The New True Size of Government*, 2006; see also Curtis W. Copeland, *The Federal Workforce: Characteristics*

and Trends (Washington, DC, Congressional Research Service, April 19, 2011), 4.

68. For one exception relevant to state government funding, see State of Florida, Office of Program Policy Analysis and Government Accountability, *Special Review: Government "Outside" Workforce Exceeds Number of State Personnel System Employees, Report No. 01-16* (Tallahassee, FL, March 2001), 1, defining "outside employees" as persons whose jobs are funded by "state contracts, grants, cooperative agreements, or direct appropriations," and estimating that "the state funded 1.33 outside jobs for every state" government employee.

69. Ibid., 1.

70. *U.S. Senate Subcommittee on Contracting Oversight, Committee on Homeland Security and Government Affairs: Hearing on Contractors: How Much Are they Costing the Government?* 112 Cong. (March 29, 2012) (testimony of Charles D. Grimes III).

71. Ibid.

72. Ibid.

73. U.S. Senate Health, Education, Labor and Pensions Committee, Majority Committee Staff Report, *Acting Responsibly? Federal Contractors Frequently Put Workers' Lives and Livelihoods at Risk* (Washington, DC, December 11, 2013), 2.

74. David G. Frederickson and H. George Frederickson, *Measuring the Performance of the Hollow State* (Washington, DC: Georgetown University Press, 2006).

75. Melvin J. Dubnick and H. George Frederickson, National Academy of Public Administration and Kettering Foundation Report, *Public Accountability: Performance Measurement, the Extended State, and the Search for Trust* (Dayton, OH: Kettering Foundation, 2011), 49.

76. Ibid., 50.

CHAPTER 4

1. Charles Murray, *In Our Hands: A Plan to Replace the Welfare State* (Washington, DC: AEI Press, 2006).

2. Arthur C. Brooks, "The Art of Limited Government," *National Affairs* no. 15 (Spring 2013): 118.

3. Ibid.

4. Michael S. Greve, "But What Kind of Federalism?" *The Insider* (Winter 2013): 12.

5. "Reagan-Carter Oct. 28, 1980, Debate – 'There You Go Again,'" You Tube video, 1:13, from the Ronald W. Reagan debate with President Jimmy Carter on October 25, 1980: posted by "MCamericanpresident," September 25, 2012, https://www.youtube.com/watch?v=qN7gDRjTNf4.

6. Ibid.

7. Paul R. Verkuil, *Outsourcing Sovereignty: How Privatization of Government Functions Threatens Democracy and What We Can Do About It* (New York: Cambridge University Press, 2007).

8. Mark H. Moore, *Creating Public Value: Strategic Management in Government* (Cambridge, MA: Harvard University Press, 1995); see also John Bennington and Mark H. Moore, eds., *Public Value: Theory and Practice* (New York: Palgrave Macmillan, 2011).

9. John D. Donohue and Richard J. Zeckhauser, *Collaborative Governance: Private Roles for Public Goals in Turbulent Times* (Princeton, NJ: Princeton University Press, 2011).

10. Stephen Goldsmith and William D. Eggers, *Governing by Network: The New Shape of the Public Sector* (Washington, DC: Brookings Institution Press, 2004); see also Stephen Goldsmith with Gigi Georges and Tim Glynn Burke, *The Power of Social Innovation: How Civic Entrepreneurs Ignite Community Networks for Good* (San Francisco: Jossey-Bass, 2010), and Elaine C. Kamarck, *The End of Government . . . As We Know It: Making Public Policy Work* (Boulder, CO: Lynne Reinner Publishers, 2007), chapter 6.

11. John J. DiIulio Jr., ed., *Deregulating the Public Service: Can Government Be Improved?* (Washington, DC: Brookings Institution Press, 1994).

12. "USDA Funds New Police Vehicle for West Wildwood," *Cape May County Herald*, August 9, 2013.

13. Jeffrey L. Pressman and Aaron Wildavsky, *Implementation: How Great Expectations in Washington Are Dashed in Oakland; Or, Why It's Amazing That Federal Programs Work at All, This Being the Saga of the Economic Development Administration as Told by Two Sympa-*

thetic Observers Who Seek to Build Morals on a Foundation of Ruined Hopes (Berkeley: University of California Press, 1973).

14. Donald F. Kettl, *Government by Proxy: (Mis?)Managing Federal Programs* (Washington, DC: Congressional Quarterly Press, 1988), 149.

15. Lester M. Salamon, "Rethinking Public Management: Third-Party Government and the Changing Forms of Government Action," *Public Policy* (Summer 1981): 255–75.

16. Harold Seidman and Robert Gilmour, *Politics, Position, and Power*, 4th ed. (New York: Oxford University Press, 1986), 128.

17. Paul C. Light, *The True Size of Government* (Washington, DC: Brookings Institution Press, 1999); see also Daniel Gutmann and Barry Willner, *The Shadow Government: The Government's Multi-Billion Dollar Giveaway of Its Decision-Making Powers to Private Management Consultants, "Experts," and Think Tanks* (New York: Pantheon, 1976).

18. H. Brinton Milward and Keith G. Provan, "Governing the Hollow State," *Journal of Public Administration Research and Theory* 10, no. 2 (2000): 359–79.

19. Melvin J. Dubnick and H. George Frederickson, National Academy of Public Administration and Kettering Foundation Report, *Public Accountability: Performance Measurement, the Extended State, and the Search for Trust* (Dayton, OH: Kettering Foundation, 2011).

20. Ibid., 42.

21. Kettl, *Government by Proxy*, 159.

22. Ibid., 161.

23. Ibid., 152–53.

24. Ibid.

25. Ibid., 154–55, 161.

CHAPTER 5

1. Seymour Martin Lipset, *The First New Nation: The United States in Historical and Comparative Perspective* (New York: W. W. Norton, 1979).

2. Peter H. Schuck and James Q. Wilson, eds., *Understanding America: The Anatomy of an Exceptional Nation* (New York: Public Affairs, 2009).

3. E. J. Dionne Jr., *Our Divided Political Heart: The Battle for the American Idea in an Age of Discontent* (New York: Bloomsbury, 2012), 5.

4. Joe Klein, "Obamacare Incompetence," *Time*, April 2, 2013.

5. Joe Klein, "Obamacare: What's True? What's False? What's Next?" (keynote address, Public Symposium on the National Field Network Study of the Affordable Care Act, University of Pennsylvania, Philadelphia, May 1, 2014).

6. Donalf F. Kettl, "The Reluctant Executive," *Government Executive*, May 9, 2014, http://www.govexec.com/magazine/features/2014/05/reluctant-executive/84109/.

7. Ibid.

8. Ibid.

9. Ibid.

10. Richard E. Neustadt, *Presidential Power: The Politics of Leadership* (New York: John Wiley & Sons, 1960), 39.

11. John J. DiIulio Jr., "Chester Alan Arthur (1881–1885)," in *Presidential Leadership: Rating the Best and the Worst in the White House*, eds. James Taranto and Leonard Leo (New York: Free Press, 2004), chapter 21.

12. Jeffrey K. Tulis, *The Rhetorical Presidency* (Princeton, NJ: Princeton University Press, 1987).

13. John J. DiIulio Jr., "The Hyper-Rhetorical Presidency," *Critical Review: A Journal of Politics and Society* 19, nos. 2–3: 315–24.

14. Alexander Hamilton, "Federalist No. 70," in *The Federalist Papers*, ed. Clinton Rossiter (New York: Signet, 1961), 421–22.

15. U.S. Census Bureau, "Population Projections, 2015–2060, Middle Series Projection for 2035: 369,662,000." Accessed March 1, 2014, and April 14, 2014. http://www.census.gov/population/projection/data.

16. Eric Katz, "Federal Agencies Shed 10,000 Jobs in March," *Government Executive*, April 4, 2014.

17. Donald F. Kettl, "From Intergovernmental to Intersectoral" (unpublished paper, 2014), 13.

18. Eric Katz, "Obama Would Increase Federal Workforce by 14,000 in 2015," *Government Executive*, March 10, 2014.

19. Independent Sector, webinars, http://www.independentsector.org/page.cfm?name=webinars, and June 18, 2014 email announcement regarding June 9, 16, and 23 training sessions.

20. National Council of Nonprofits, *Toward Common Sense Contracting: What Taxpayers Deserve* (Washington, DC, 2014), 49.

21. U.S. Census Bureau, *Statistical Abstract of the United States: 2012* (Washington, DC, 2012), 269, table 432.

22. White House, *Economic Report of the President, Transmitted to the Congress March 2013 Together with the Annual Report of the Council of Economic Advisers* (Washington, DC, March 2013), 114, figure 3-13, showing that in constant 2005 dollars total federal grants to state and local governments rose from $45.3 billion in 1960 to $504.4 billion in 2012.

23. Alice Rivlin, "Rethinking Federalism for More Effective Governance," *Publius: The Journal of Federalism* 42, no. 3 (2012): 393.

CHAPTER 7

1. M. Olson, *The Logic of Collective Action: Public Goods and the Theory of Groups* (Cambridge, MA: Harvard University Press, 1965).

2. M. Olson, *The Rise and Decline of Nations: Economic Growth, Stagflation, and Social Rigidities* (New Haven, CT: Yale University Press, 1982).

3. Joe Weisenthal, "The Four Things That Worry Jamie Dimon," *Business Insider*, February 4, 2013, http://www.businessinsider.com/the-four-things-that-worry-jamie-dimon-2013-2#ixzz2JwAGvxIo.

4. J. Rauch, *Government's End: Why Washington Stopped Working* (New York: Public Affairs, 1999).

5. In addition to Rauch's *Government's End*, these titles will get interested readers started: F. H. Buckley, ed., *The American Illness: Essays on the Rule of Law* (New Haven, CT: Yale University Press, 2013); G. Healy, ed., *Go Directly to Jail: The Criminalization of Almost Everything* (Washington, DC: Cato Institute, 2004); R. Levy, *Shakedown: How Corporations, Government, and Trial Lawyers Abuse the Judicial Process* (Washington, DC: Cato Institute, 2004); H. A. Silverglate, *Three Felonies a Day: How the Feds Target the Innocent* (New York: Encounter, 2011); J. V. Delong, *Out of Bounds Out of Control: Regulatory Enforcement at the EPA* (Washington, DC: Cato Institute, 2002). Other books on more specific topics are Sean Farhang's *The*

Litigation State, Gene Healy's *Go Directly to Jail*, and Walter Olson's *The Litigation Explosion* and *The Rule of Lawyers*.

6. Jonathan Lister, "OSHA Regulations Pertaining to Grocery Store Operations," *Houston Chronicle*, http://smallbusiness.chron.com/osha-regulations-pertaining-to-grocery-store-operations-37571.html.

7. OSHA Manuals for Physicians, Dentists, and Veternarians. "Products." http://www.oshamanual.com/dental_osha.html?gclid=CO Cwv--oirsCFdE-MgodlTkAzA.

8. Partnership for Public Service and Booz Allen Hamilton, *Building the Enterprise: A New Civil Service Framework* (Washington, DC, April 2014).

9. Ibid., 8.

10. Ibid.

Epilogue

1. See my reference in chapter 5 to the wonderful book by E. J. Dionne Jr., *Our Divided Political Heart: The Battle for the American Idea in an Age of Discontent* (New York: Bloomsbury, 2012).

2. John J. DiIulio Jr., "Why I Am Still a Democrat," *The Claremont Review*, Winter 2012/2013, 71–72.

3. Bradley D. Nash and Cornelius Lynde, *A Hook in Leviathan: A Critical Interpretation of the Hoover Commission Report* (New York: Macmillan, 1950), 186.

4. John Micklethwait, "Taming Leviathan: A Special Report on the Future of the State," *The Economist*, March 19, 2011.

5. For instance, see John J. DiIulio Jr., "The Moral Compassion of True Conservatism," in *The Fractious Nation? Unity and Division in Contemporary American Life*, ed. Jonathan Reidel (Berkeley: University of California Press, 2003), chapter 13, and John J. DiIulio Jr. "Attacking Sinful Inequalities," *Perspectives on Politics*, December 2004, 651, 667–70.

6. U.S. Office of Management and Budget, *Budget of the United States Fiscal Year 2013, Historical Tables, Summary of Receipts, Outlays, and Surpluses or Deficits* (Washington, DC, 2012), 137–38, table 6.1; Benjamin Zycher, *State and Local Spending: Do Tax and Expenditure Limits Work? American Enterprise Institute*, May 2013, 6–7, table 1;

John Micklewaite, "Taming Leviathan," 4.

7. "More Americans Relying on Government Benefits," *New York Times*, February 11, 2012, http://www.nytimes.com/interactive/2012/02/12/us/relying-on-government-benefits.html.

8. The Heritage Foundation, Center for Data Analysis Report, *The 2010 Index of Dependence on Government* (Washington, DC, October 14, 2010), 1.

9. Alexis de Tocqueville, *Democracy in America, Vol. II*, ed. Phillips Bradley (New York: Alfred A. Knopf, 1991), 318–19.

10. Ibid.

11. I am developing these and related Tocqueville-inspired themes and theses for a book that parses and probes the historic rise of "big government" in America and forecasts the problems that it will pose by the middle of the present century (problems that will emerge even if we hire a million more federal bureaucrats by 2035 and take the other measures proposed in the present treatise). This book will explore the subject in relation to relevant academic literature including, but not limited to, the literature in political science on American political development; see *The Daddy State: Facing Up to Big Government*, forthcoming (I hope!) in 2016 from Princeton University Press.

12. Tocqueville, *Democracy*, 319.

13. See my reference in chapter 4 to the fascinating book by Charles Murray, *In Our Hands: A Plan to Replace the Welfare State* (Washington, DC: AEI Press, 2006).

14. Jonathan Rauch, *Government's End: Why Washington Stopped Working* (New York: PublicAffairs, 1999).

15. Jonathan Rauch, *Demosclerosis: The Silent Killer of American Government* (New York: Time Books, 1994).

16. James Q. Wilson, *Political Organizations* (Princeton, NJ: Princeton University Press, 1995), 23–25; see also James Q. Wilson, *Bureaucracy: What Government Agencies Do and Why They Do It* (New York: Basic Books, 1989).

17. R. Douglas Arnold, *The Logic of Congressional Action* (New Haven, CT: Yale University Press, 1992).

18. Theodore J. Lowi, *The End of Liberalism: The Second Republic of the United States* (New York: W. W. Norton, 1969).

19. John J. DiIulio Jr., "Principled Agents: The Cultural Bases of Behavior in a Federal Government Bureaucracy," *Journal of Public Administration Research and Theory* 4, no. 3 (1994): 277–317.

20. Donald F. Kettl et al., *Civil Service Reform: Building a Government That Works* (Washington, DC: Brookings Institution Press, 1996).

21. Ibid., 20–21.

About the Contributors

―――――――――― ⋙⋘ ――――――――――

JOHN J. DIIULIO JR. is the Frederic Fox Leadership Professor of Politics, Religion, and Civil Society and professor of political science at the University of Pennsylvania. He has directed research centers at the Brookings Institution and other think tanks and has taught American government at several universities including Penn, Harvard, and Princeton. A member of the National Academy of Public Administration, he served as first director of the White House Office of Faith-Based and Community Initiatives.

E. J. DIONNE JR. is a columnist for the *Washington Post*, senior fellow at the Brookings Institution, and University Professor in the Foundations of Democracy and Culture at Georgetown's McCourt School of Public Policy. He is the author, most recently, of *Our Divided Political Heart*.

CHARLES MURRAY is a political scientist, author, and libertarian. He first came to national attention in 1984 with the publication of *Losing Ground*, which has been credited as the intellectual foundation for the Welfare Reform Act of 1996. His 1994 *New York Times* bestseller, *The Bell Curve*, coauthored with the late Richard J. Herrnstein, sparked heated controversy for its analysis of the role of IQ in shaping America's class structure. Murray's other books include *What It Means to Be a Libertarian*, *Human Accomplishment*, *In Our Hands*, and *Real Education*. His most recent book, *Coming Apart*, describes an unprecedented divergence in American classes over the last half-century.